THE ENIGMA OF SHORT PARENTS WHO HAVE TALL CHILDREN:
THE NPA MODEL OF GENETIC TRAITS

THE ENIGMA OF SHORT PARENTS WHO HAVE TALL CHILDREN: THE NPA MODEL OF GENETIC TRAITS

A.M. BENIS, Sc.D., M.D.

A.M. BENIS
New York

When you cannot measure it, when you cannot express it in numbers, you have scarcely, in your thoughts, advanced to the stage of Science, whatever the matter may be.

— Lord Kelvin (1883)

We are standing at the threshold of an era in which the entire proud edifice of medicine — including psychiatry as a whole as well as psychoanalysis — will rest on genetics.

— Sandor Rado (1961)

CONTENTS

Preface   ix

CHAP. 1: Personality and Physical Stature   1

CHAP. 2: The NPA Model of Personality   9

CHAP. 3: NPA Dominant Types   17

CHAP. 4: Inheritance of the NPA Traits   27

CHAP. 5: Typing People   33

CHAP. 6: Case Studies & the Solution to the Puzzle   37

CHAP. 7: Conclusion   45

Appendix: Synopsis of NPA Theory   49

Glossary   69

References & Notes   73

Bibliography   76

Sources of Illustrations   77

Acknowledgement   78

About the Author   79

ILLUSTRATIONS & TABLES

CHAP. 1: Personality and Physical Stature

    Fig. 1. Personality types of antiquity

    Fig. 2: Tall bridal couple with parents

CHAP. 2: The NPA Model of Personality

    Fig. 3. The sanguine smile

    Fig. 4. Faces in rage

CHAP. 3: NPA Dominant Types

    Fig. 5. Caricatures: Dominant types

    Fig. 6. Caricatures: the tall NP type (Abraham Lincoln)

CHAP. 4: Inheritance of the NPA Traits

    Table 1. Genotypes of the Dominant types

    Table 2. Types in offspring according to parents

    Table 3. Genotypes of non-viable types

    Table 4. Types in offspring including non-viable types

CHAP. 6: Case Studies & the Solution to the Puzzle

    Table 5. "The Table"

APPENDIX: Synopsis of NPA Theory

    Fig. A1. Venn diagram of Dominant types

    Fig. A2. Karen Horney

    Fig. A3. Character types of antiquity

    Fig. A4. Olive baboon: a PA type

    Table A1. Phenotypes in offspring

    Table A2. Phenotypes based on gene frequencies

    Table A3. Phenotype frequencies in subpopulations

PREFACE

As the title suggests, the purpose of this book is to solve an enigma that has been puzzling geneticists for decades: how is it possible that some parents who are short or normal in stature can have multiple children who are much taller. Perhaps you are a member of a family where this has occurred. In that case, you have already heard comments like "Wow! Where did those genes come from?" Or, perhaps you have heard the explanation that "Uncle Henry on your mother's side was tall, so you and your sisters must all have his gene..." as if Uncle Henry could somehow directly, mysteriously and faithfully pass on "his gene" to you and your siblings while bypassing your mother.

The solution to our puzzle comes from an unlikely source: the "NPA" model of personality based on three genetic traits. We use the quantitative relationships inherent in the model to postulate a genetic explanation for how physical stature is determined in some families where the children are tall.

Notice that we emphasize *in some families*. This is very much a family affair, where an unusual convergence of genes takes place. We do not mean to say that the genetic mechanism that we propose is necessarily an important facet of the genetic basis of physical stature in any particular population at large.

Given that you are probably unfamiliar with the NPA model, we have included in Chaps. 2 to 5 a fairly complete introduction to the quantitative aspects of the model. Here, you will find all of the key elements of the theory: the NPA traits, the personality types, as well as tables showing how the traits are transmitted from parents to child. The NPA model is based on classical genetics, so use of some symbols, charts and computations has been unavoidable. However, the concepts are not difficult to understand and should be amenable to the general reader.

The three NPA traits of sanguinity, perfectionism and aggression were first advanced as a group by Karen Horney in the 1950's ("We must consider at least three subdivisions of the 'expansive type': the narcissistic, the perfectionistic and the arrogant-vindictive type.") Horney's interpretation of her three types was that they were the result of stressful *environment*, but this is understandable, since her training was in psychoanalysis, and the age of genetics had not yet arrived. If Horney had lived to our more modern era, it is likely that she would have embraced a genetic explanation for the three traits. Very likely, she would have found satisfaction in the idea that they are not maladaptive reactions due to onerous environment, but rather basic structural elements of the human personality.

Your main interest in the subject considered here may have been in the realm of "physical stature", rather than "genetic personality traits". But perhaps the two are related. For some individuals the NPA model has been an exciting journey, and perhaps the same will be true for you as well.

AMB
27 August 2018

1

Personality and Physical Stature

HUMAN personality and human physique are complex entities, each having the genetic and environmental underpinnings of "nature" and "nurture". In both cases, the inheritance is "polygenic", meaning that more than one gene is involved in their expression.

Since the middle of the past century, a possible genetic association of personality with physique has been controversial, most likely because they are very personal entities: an individual's successful social functioning is highly dependent both on one's personality traits and on physical stature. In the absence of crisp studies pinpointing specific genes, it has always been more comforting to default to the politically correct notion that it is the environmental factors that are the overriding influences — i.e., factors that we can conveniently modify if we choose to do so.

The purpose of this book is to solve a particular puzzle, and in doing so, to introduce to you a general theory of personality that you can apply to your own personal life. As you may have surmised from the book's title, the puzzle that we need to solve is the following:

How is it possible that two parents who are of short or normal stature can have multiple children who are all tall?

And by "tall" we do not mean just a little bit taller than the parents, but sometimes even by six inches (15 cm) or more. And not in just one child, but in two… three… four children, in succession.

Even if one acknowledges that "many genes" may be involved in the determination of stature, something seems odd here. How do the children in these families seemingly always select out the "tall genes" that seem to be hiding in their parents' genomes?

Granted that a family with short parents and tall children is an unusual occurrence, the fact that such families do exist begs an explanation nonetheless. In the pages below, we set out to solve the "short parents – tall children" puzzle, and we invite the reader to join us. The solution has not yet been verified by geneticists, so we cannot guarantee that it is correct. But, it is a remarkably simple one, and if this is a subject that interests you, we can guarantee you an interesting, if not exciting, sojourn.

Personality

Personality is a notoriously complex entity, and there have been a multitude of efforts to define and measure it. Most definitions of personality are something like "a collection of emotional, thought and behavioral patterns unique to a person that is consistent over time" [1].

It is common knowledge that personality traits are, to a degree, heritable. Everybody knows that identical twins are not only "identical" with regard to physical features, but similar in personality as well. And everyone knows instances where a child is a "spitting image" of one of the parents. And by this it is meant that the son or daughter not only looks like, but remarkably behaves like one of the parents.

Scientifically speaking, personality research has not made much progress in the past decades. Many theories of personality have been advanced, which means that there is no consensus as to which approach is the correct one. Most of the concepts are fuzzy and empirical and not amenable to being either proved or disproved.

As things stand at present, the conventional wisdom of the research community is that *many genes* contribute to personality, and the complexity is such that *no gene* contributes more than a few percent of the effect in any aspect of human behavior. As a result, there is currently little effort being made to identify specific genetic traits and to incorporate them into a model of personality. Conventional wisdom has firmly established the politically correct illusion that the human personality is so complex that every child is effectively a "blank slate" at birth, capable of being molded into any conceivable configuration by parental nurture, education or other aspects of environment.

Unfortunately, the above conventional wisdom is quite wrong, and it will eventually be shown to be false by geneticists, probably in the not too distant future. In fact, we can easily show that it is false from common experience. We all know of instances where a child has a "personality type" just like one of the parents — who themselves may be very different. It is a very common occurrence. There are striking examples of this in my family and probably in yours as well. Now, if *many genes* were involved, a child's inheriting the "entire packet" of personality genes from just one of the parents would be an extremely rare event! After all, the "many" genes would be scattered on that parent's more than twenty pairs of chromosomes, and since a child inherits only one chromosome of each pair, how could all of the "many genes" be transmitted together to provide a "spitting image" of one parent?

Our premise is that despite the complexity of the fine details of personality, the basic structure of an individual's personality type is determined by only three genetic traits acting together.

The three-trait model

Our NPA model is the only "trait model of personality" proposed to date that is based on classical genetics. In our experience, the model corresponds closely to reality and explains why so often a child's personality is so similar to that of one of the parents. However, the NPA traits have not yet been researched

[*J.K. Lavater, ca. 1775*]

Fig. 1. Personality types according to the ancient theory of humors: *Phlegmaticus, Cholericus, Sanguineus* and *Melancholicus.*

by geneticists, so any results that the model produces must be cautiously termed as theoretical or provisional. But the potential of the NPA model is unique: it is the only theory of personality that proposes to make an assessment of the personality types of children according to the personality types of the parents.

The model was developed on the basis of concepts clarified over sixty years ago by psychiatrist Karen Horney. According to the model, there are three major character traits that form the basis of personality. The traits are *sanguinity* (N), *perfectionism* (P) and *aggression* (A). The traits are multifaceted, or in formal terms, each one dependent on a "pleiotropic gene" by which a single gene can cause a complex pattern of aspects related to behavior.

The letter N is used to denote sanguinity because it is related to the classic concept of "narcissism". The two traits, A and N, represent the fundamental basis of the human personality structure. Every individual must have a measure of trait A, or trait N, or both.

The genetic basis of an individual's *NPA personality type* is determined by the combination of N, P and A traits that he or she has inherited from the parents. There are about a dozen common NPA personality types.

The concept that humans have a limited number of discrete character types is not new. Hippocrates in the fourth century B.C. developed a concept of character types based on excesses of body fluids, or "humors". The types emerged under the labels of *Sanguine, Choleric, Phlegmatic* and *Melancholic* (see Fig. 1). These types are very close to the personality types generated by the NPA model, especially if one appreciates that the Sanguine and Choleric types represent the fundamental traits of sanguinity and aggression, and that the Phlegmatic and Melancholic types are composites that involve the third trait of the NPA model, perfectionism.

[*Katherine Hala*]

Fig. 2. An American "bridal couple with their parents". In this book we attempt solve the enigma of why, in some families, parents of short or normal stature can have multiple children who are considerably taller.

Physical stature

Like personality, physical stature is mostly inherited, although environmental factors, like nutrition, can sometimes be very important. Recent "genome-wide association studies" have revealed hundreds of genetic loci that may influence human stature, these genes being distinct from those related to gender or to medical conditions such as endocrine abnormalities. As in the case of personality, the conventional wisdom is that many genes influence stature, but that no identifiable gene has a great effect.

As in the case of personality, the conventional wisdom appears to be wrong once again. This can be inferred from families in which the parents are of normal stature, while the children are either of normal height or very tall. The appearance of multiple children who are very tall alongside those of normal height implies that only a few genes, either dominant or recessive, are causing a marked effect on stature *in that particular family* and that the tall stature in those children is not the result of the confluence of "many genes" gathered from both parents.

The association of personality and physical stature

Inquiry into possible interrelationships between personality on the one hand, and human physique, stature or physiognomy on the other hand is not something new. Even the ancients ascribed characteristics of physique to their four character types of the "theory of humors" (Fig. 1), and in the mid-twentieth century, individuals like psychiatrist Ernst Kretschmer in Germany and psychologist William Sheldon in the United States advanced theories of body types ("somatotypes") that were supposedly correlated with personality, mental disease, intelligence and whatnot. Unfortunately, the findings of these researchers in that new field of "constitutional psychology" became mired in controversies of politics, racism and eugenics, so that their claims have been largely dismissed by modern scientists, being considered to be outdated or even tinged with "quackery". As things stand now, this field is dormant, and few genetic researchers today would risk their careers by considering the topic to be one meriting serious scientific inquiry. Once again, the conventional wisdom is that there are no reliable links between physical stature and personality traits.

The NPA model and physical stature

Our NPA model is primarily a model of personality traits based on genes. However, the model does not summarily reject the possibility that certain genetic personality types may be associated with body physique, physical stature and even with physiognomy, such as facial features and the capacity to exhibit a social smile. A single gene can sometimes have multiple effects on the structure and function of an organism (known as "pleiotropism" in genetics). And sometimes genes interact together as "complementary genes" to produce unusual effects. There is no reason why we should *a priori* dismiss the possibility that in some families there is a strong genetic link between personality and physical stature. Perhaps the negativistic conventional wisdom is wrong here, too.

The scope of this book

Our aim is a concise presentation of the essential elements of our approach — in terms of genetics — to solve the enigma of how parents who are of short stature can have multiple children who are very tall.

In the chapters that follow, we present:

- Our model of personality based on the three traits: N, P and A.

- A brief description of the Dominant personality types generated by the model.

- Quantitative aspects of the model, namely of how the NPA traits are transmitted from parent to child.

- How the NPA types of individuals can be identified in the real world in the absence of genetic testing.

- Case studies of families with short parents and tall children, leading to a hypothesis for a genetic mechanism for this phenomenon… and to the solution of our puzzle.

- Concluding remarks and Summary.

2

The NPA Model of Personality

The NPA model of personality was developed on the basis of concepts advanced by German-American psychiatrist Karen Horney during the mid-twentieth century [2]. According to the theory, there are three major genetically determined character traits that form the basis of personality. The traits are *sanguinity* (N), *perfectionism* (P) and *aggression* (A).

An important premise of the model is that in any individual either the trait N or A, or both, must be expressed.

The three traits

Sanguinity (N) is the trait of sociability. Individuals with the trait tend to be prone to flushing, blushing and tearfulness. A hallmark of the trait is the *gingival smile* (Fig. 3) broadly exposing gums and teeth [3]. In the extreme, the trait appears as a "search for glory", and individuals may display vanity, exhibitionism and show overt narcissistic behavior. Individuals having trait N are called "sanguine" types and sometimes, appropriately, "narcissistic" types.

Aggression (A) is the well-known trait of competitiveness, often physical in nature. Individuals having the A trait (but lacking the N trait) tend to be inhibited in sociability and in

[*Max.thinks.sees*]

Fig. 3. Physiognomy of the N trait: the gingival smile. In the model, we posit that the N trait is transmitted from parents to child by recessive genetics.

flushing, blushing, tearfulness and smiling. In the extreme, the trait is a "search for power", and individuals may display physical confrontation, pugnacity and show overtly sadistic behavior. Individuals with the trait of aggression instinctively form "pecking orders". Individuals having trait A but lacking trait N are called "non-sanguine" types.

Perfectionism (P) is a trait that may or may not be present in a given individual. It may be thought of as modulating the "unbridled" N and A traits. Individuals having overt expression of the P trait tend to value order, neatness and symmetry, and may be prone to repetitive mannerisms. In the extreme, the trait may be the cause of obsessive-compulsive or autistic-like behavior that may overwhelm other character traits. Individuals lacking trait P are called "non-perfectionistic".

Traits A and N are associated with rage reactions, namely the classic "aggressive-vindictive rage" (A rage) associated with pallor in individuals of light skin color, and the florid "narcissistic rage" (N rage) associated with sanguinity. The P trait is not associated with a rage reaction.

The traits A and N form the basis of human ambition, namely the desire to achieve power and glory, respectively.

An important result is that the model produces a limited number of discrete character types, according to how the three traits are assorted, and whether the traits are present, absent, or incompletely expressed. In this book, we shall concentrate on *Dominant types,* in which the three traits are transmitted independently from parents to child and are fully expressed.

1. Dominant types

In the case that all three traits are either absent or fully expressed, we obtain the following types:

N   sanguine

A   non-sanguine aggressive

NA   sanguine aggressive

NP   sanguine perfectionistic

PA   non-sanguine perfectionistic aggressive

NPA   sanguine perfectionistic aggressive

Types are denoted *sanguine* or *non-sanguine* depending on the presence or absence of the trait N, respectively. The two Dominant non-sanguine types are A and PA.

Types are denoted *aggressive* or *non-aggressive* depending on the presence or absence of the trait A. The two Dominant non-aggressive types are N and NP.

Thus, there are four sanguine and two non-sanguine Dominant types, as well as four aggressive and two non-aggressive Dominant types.

2. Other types of the model

There are several other categories of character types in the NPA model. These are 1) the Passive Aggressive and Resigned types, in which the A trait is partially inhibited, and 2) the Borderline types, in which neither trait N nor A is fully expressed.

In order to avoid making our analysis needlessly complicated, we confine our discussion here to the Dominant types of the model. For further information about the other types, see the Appendix.

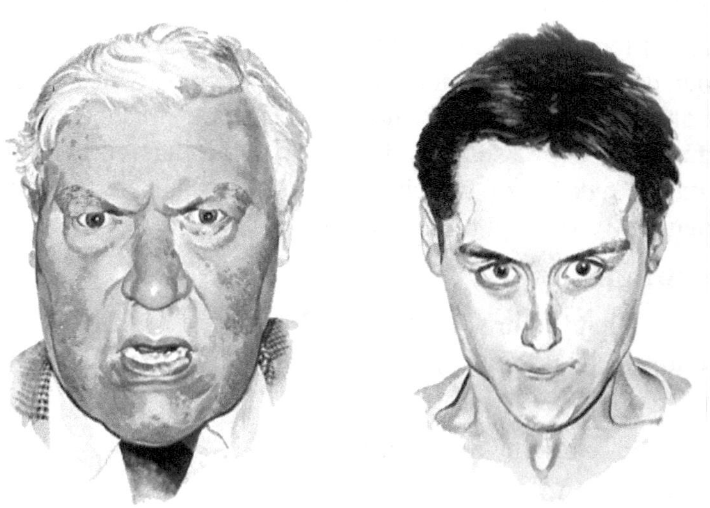

[*A. Moore*]

Fig. 4. Faces in rage: the "N rage" in a sanguine type, and "A rage" in a non-sanguine type.

The N and A rages

The occurrence of the N and A rages is possible in any of the types having the N and A traits, respectively (Fig. 4). The rages are typically triggered by stressful environmental circumstances during an individual's daily life. The two rages can occur together, synergistically, in the "NA rage" if both the N and A traits are present in the individual's type, as for example in the NA and NPA types.

The non-aggressive N and NP types are genetically inhibited from exhibiting the A rage of aggression, just as the non-sanguine A and PA types lack the capacity to exhibit the N rage of sanguinity.

Complexities: other genes and environment

Biological variability and outliers

Just as all males and all females are not alike, there is considerable variability in the behavioral characteristics of a given genetic NPA type. This is basically because of 1) "genes other than the NPA genes" that influence behavior, and 2) environment.

In the extreme, one should be aware that "outliers" can certainly exist. An outlier is an individual of a certain NPA type who has some unusual attributes that seem "out of character" for that particular type. There are two main reasons for outliers. First, the individual may have an unusual "other gene" that rarely occurs in the general population, or the individual may have been exposed to an unusual set of environmental conditions. Second, the individual may simply have an unusual combination, or "perfect storm", of commonly occurring genes or environmental exposures.

Thus, the NPA traits are only a basic structural skeleton of the human personality, with many other factors, both genetic and environmental, possibly contributing to biological variability in the various NPA types. Among these are *basic drives* (hunger, thirst, sex, territoriality), *cognition* (thinking, learning, reasoning, intelligence), *temperament* (the natural activity or excitability of an individual), as well as other less clearly defined human traits, like empathy and altruism. *Environmental variables* like nurture, culture, and the individual's real-life situation in society provide a final overlay of complexity.

Temperament as a facet of personality

One of the most important aspects of the genetics of personality in the category of "genes other than the NPA genes" is the notion of temperament. By this, we mean the *general activity or reactivity* of an individual, in the sense that it is applied with regard to domesticated animals, such as dogs or horses. Thus, a particular individual, say an NP type, could be described as having a "high temperament" or a "low temperament".

The concept of temperament has not been adequately investigated, or even appreciated, in the behavioral sciences. In the NPA model we make the simplest assumption: that the genes that underlie temperament are separate from the NPA genes, hence that the NPA personality type of an individual can be determined irrespective of his or her innate level of temperament.

The "television set" analogy

One can think of an individual's personality in terms of the analogy of viewing a television receiver. If there were only two basic models of television sets, then this would represent the *male-female dichotomy*: Then, the *NPA personality type* would then be the channel selector, *temperament* would be the volume control, and how well the TV picture is actually visualized would depend on the lighting in the room, or *environment*.

While acknowledging the complexity of personality in the broader sense of the term, including the above concept of temperament, the model implies that it is the *male-female dichotomy* and the *NPA personality type* that comprise the highest genetic tiers of the human personality structure. Specifically, despite the complexities of "biological variability" and temperament , we can, in principle, identify an individual's unique genetic NPA type.

Profiles of the NPA types

In next chapter, we summarize profiles of the Dominant NPA character types. The profiles are excerpts from our prior work [4], where the descriptions were presented mainly in the form of *caricatures*. The reason for the use of caricatures was that it allowed us to focus on the specific characteristics, and foibles, of the various NPA types without any implication that the descriptions are to be taken literally or pejoratively.

Despite our appreciation of the complications of "biological variability", we have in the various NPA types observed trends for such categories as *complexion, gestures, handwriting, physical stature*, and so on. One of the trends that we observed early in developing the NPA model was the frequent occurrence of short and tall stature in some of the NPA Dominant types [5]. We shall put those observations to good use in the pages that follow.

[*DonkeyHotey & Carsten S.*]

Fig. 5. Caricatures of the six Dominant types. *L to R, from top:* N, A, NP, PA, NPA and NA.

3

The Dominant NPA Types

The main category of the NPA types of the model is that of the *Dominant types,* where all three traits are either absent or fully expressed. Thus, there are six Dominant types:

N   sanguine

A   non-sanguine aggressive

NA   sanguine aggressive

NP   sanguine perfectionistic

PA   non-sanguine perfectionistic aggressive

NPA   sanguine perfectionistic aggressive

The N, NA, NP and NPA types are the *sanguine* types, meaning that they have the N trait. The A and PA types are called *non-sanguine* types.

The A, NA, PA and NPA are the *aggressive* types, meaning that they have the A trait. The N and NP types are called *non-aggressive* types.

The NP, PA and NPA types are the *perfectionistic* types, meaning that they have the P trait. The N, A and NA types are called *non-perfectionistic* types. These latter three types, where neither trait N nor A is tempered by the P trait, are prone to what we term "unbridled narcissism" or "unbridled aggression".

The pure N and A types

The N type and the A type may be regarded to be "pure" types, in the sense that they are the only types having just a single NPA trait that is not influenced by the other two traits. Thus, the traits of sanguinity and aggression can be best appreciated in the N and A types. In these typically extroverted individuals we can appreciate the unfettered extremes of human behavior that have their roots in the N and A traits. For the N trait, these extremes lie in vanity, exhibitionism and narcissism, or "narcissistic personality disorder". For the A trait, the extremes lie in coerciveness, brutishness and sadism, or "antisocial personality disorder".

The N and A traits together

The N and A traits are present together, fully expressed, in the NA type. The two traits tend not to interfere with each other, or modify each other. Rather, they appear together in an unchanged or synergistic manner, so that the NA type is typically an active, highly extroverted, non-perfectionistic individual where full-blown "unbridled" narcissism and aggression are often both on display.

The bridling effect of the P trait: NP and PA types

The effect of the presence of the P trait on the N and A traits can be profound. The effect on the N trait is such that instead of an outgoing N individual prone to vanity, the result is a less extroverted NP individual prone to perfectionistic introspection and even obsessive compulsiveness. The effect on the A trait is such that instead of an outgoing A individual prone to overt brutishness, the result is a less extroverted PA individual prone to repressed aggressive behavior.

When all three N, P and A traits are present

The individual having all three traits together, fully expressed, is the NPA dominant type. The resultant effect of the three traits being present together may be appreciated by imagining "adding the P trait" to the behavior of the NA type. The effect is a tempering one, but the result is still an extroverted individual who may be prone to excesses characteristic of the both the N and A traits acting in concert. The outward effects of the N and A traits may be so overt that although these individuals may consider themselves to be "perfectionists", this may not be the opinion of others. That is, the N and A traits acting together may mask the presence of the P trait as a modulating trait in the sense of "perfectionism".

Below are brief profiles of the six Dominant types:

N type

"Sanguine type"

Sanguine, non-perfectionistic, non-aggressive type

N types are typically extroverted, sanguine complexioned, non-perfectionistic, and prone to narcissistic posturing and adornment. Low temperament individuals can be soft-spoken, gallant or angelic. High temperament individuals can be charismatic, or intrusive, overbearing and brash. The N type is quite common in politics, aristocratic families and in all lists of famous people, especially in the arts.

Rage: Narcissistic "N rage" (florid rage resembling a childish tantrum).

Also known as: "Narcissistic type". Charismatic personality. The self-anointed glory seeker. The show-off. "Narcissus".

Complexion: Sanguine, florid, flushed to blood-red in individuals of light skin color. Blushes easily.

Smile: Radiant "gingival" smile, broadly exposing gums and teeth.

Photograph: Looks at camera. Broad charismatic gingival smile. Starry-eyed smile.

Voice: Confident, smooth, unctuous, pontificating.

Gestures: Deep bow, accompanied by sweeping arm. "Narcissistic arms gesture" in which the arms are extended to the front or sides, with the palms up and the fingers somewhat spread apart. It is a pose often assumed by singers and by religious leaders. "Joan of Arc pose" in which the individual's eyes are directed toward the heavens when accepting recognition in the limelight.

Handwriting: Very variable. May be beautifully well formed with flourishes, but non-perfectionistic. May be illegible scribbling, especially in male. Exhibitionistic signature ("John Hancock") is common.

Color preference: Red, especially deep red, is the favorite color of the N type.

A type

"Aggressive type"

Non-sanguine, non-perfectionistic, aggressive type

A types typically have a non-sanguine complexion, are extroverted, brusque, brash and prone to aggressive-vindictive arrogance, but not exhibitionistic or narcissistic. The female is sometimes denigrated as "masculine". Circumstances can lead this type to be overtly sadistic. A positive attribute is that he or she gets things done and gets them done fast. Short physical stature is common but not universal.

Rage: Aggressive-vindictive "A rage" (mass discharge of sympathetic nervous system). Also called the "fight or flight" response.

Also known as: Aggressive, choleric personality. "The arrogant dynamo". Non-sanguine autocrat.

Complexion: Non-sanguine. Tending toward pallid or sallow in individuals of light skin color. May be milky white. Does not blush easily.

Smile: Sardonic smirk. Non-gingival, half-open mouthed grin. Grin with short, repetitive laugh to mask the incapacity to smile.

Photograph: Looks at camera. "Pleased-with-self" grin.

Voice: Confident, confrontational, abrasive, bullying.

Gestures: Clenched fist, aggressive finger point, haughtily-cocked jaw, intimidating glare.

Handwriting: Non-perfectionistic. Often slurred or bold illegible scrawl.

Color preference: Inattentive approach to color choice.

NA type

"Sanguine-aggressive type"

Sanguine, non-perfectionistic, aggressive type

NA types tend to be sanguine-complexioned, hyperactive extroverts. Both traits of ambition, i.e., "unbridled" narcissism and aggression, are fully manifest. NA individuals may be characterized by intemperate behavior not conducive to stable relationships. If the trait of aggression predominates, then the NA type may exhibit sadistic behavior. The NA type often seeks celebrity status, especially in the performing arts.

Rage: Narcissistic "N rage" or aggressive "A rage" or combined "NA rage".

Also known as: "Narcissistic-aggressive type". Cyclothymic, histrionic, hysterical or hypomanic-depressive personality. "The ambitious predator". The *prima donna*.

Complexion: Tending toward sanguine or flushed in individuals of light skin color. NA types have the capacity to blush but typically are unembarrassable.

Smile: Showy, glamorous smile of a movie star.

Photograph: Looks at camera. Extroverted, flashy smile.

Voice: Confident. Highly-modulated with mini-bursts of rapid-fire speech.

Gestures: Active or hyperactive gestures. Often seductive body contact in casual social situations.

Handwriting: Variable, non-perfectionistic. Sometimes rounded, elegant letters in female.

Color preference: Bright yellow, pink, orange, multicolors. Even chartreuse. No particular attraction to red.

Fig. 6. "Honest Abe" Lincoln. Caricature of the tall, lean, perfectionistic, industrious NP type. Not all NP types fit this stereotype of the "ectomorphic" body type, but this physique does appear frequently in the NP personality type of European heritage.

NP type

"Sanguine-perfectionistic type"

Sanguine, perfectionistic, non-aggressive type

NP types are usually reserved, unaggressive individuals, tending toward a sanguine complexion and a propensity to blush easily. The N trait of sanguinity is "bridled" by the P trait, so overt narcissism is absent. This is the dutiful, aloof individual who is obsessive and compulsive with regard to order, symmetry and neatness. Despite being unaggressive, these individuals can be very stubborn. Low temperament individuals may be described as "melancholic", while high temperament individuals can be "nervous birds" and may be more sociable. Tall and lean physical stature is common but not universal.

Rage: Narcissistic "N rage".

Also known as: "Narcissistic-perfectionist type". Obsessive-compulsive personality. Phlegmatic-melancholic or bovine personality. "Nervous bird" personality. "The aloof achiever".

Complexion: Tending toward sanguine or flushed in individuals of light skin color. Prone to blush very easily.

Smile: Uncommon sudden warm, radiant sheepish smile. Sometimes gingival smile (broadly exposing gums and teeth). The gingival smile is striking when seen, but may be rare, especially in melancholic individuals.

Photograph: Looks at camera. Relaxed face; sheepish, sometimes radiant "limelight" smile.

Voice: Confident, measured, deferential.

Gestures: Sometimes "narcissistic arms" gesture in which the arms are extended in front of the individual, with palms up and the fingers somewhat spread apart. It is a pose often assumed by singers and by religious leaders when praising their gods.

Handwriting: Almost invariably well-formed, with each letter clearly legible. Sometimes striking calligraphic quality. Sometimes tiny, well-formed letters.

Color preference: Subdued colors. Dark blue, black, white, black-and-white, beige. Tends to avoid bright red, especially in female.

PA type

"Perfectionist-aggressive type"

Non-sanguine, perfectionistic, aggressive type

PA types tend to a non-sanguine complexion. Individuals of low temperament can be well-adjusted stodgy, dutiful, socially conscious "solid citizens". Higher temperament individuals can be somewhat stern or haughty extroverts. If the PA type comes to absolute power, then overt sadistic trends may come to the fore. The PA type is relatively uncommon in the USA and Western Europe but common in the Middle East, Eastern Europe and western Russia.

Rage: Aggressive "A rage".

Also known as: Reserved aggressive personality. Austere melancholic or paranoid personality. Pseudo-narcissistic extrovert. "The sardonic wit". "The suspicious manipulator". "The Power behind the throne".

Complexion: Non-sanguine. Tending toward sallow, pallid or milky white in individuals with light skin color. Does not blush easily.

Smile: Non-symmetric grin or grimace. Mona Lisa "smile". Sardonic smirk. Frozen, toothy but non-gingival grin. Half open-mouthed grin. Grin with short repetitive laugh.

Photograph: Usually looks at camera. May pompously look away from camera. Not relaxed. No smile, half smile, tight-lipped sardonic smile, non-symmetric grin or grimace. Laughs or tries to laugh, showing expressive extroverted countenance.

Voice: Confident, contentious, measured, dispassionate.

Gestures: Upraised clenched fist, the haughtily cocked jaw, the furrowed brow, the strained tight-lipped mouth and the intimidating glare.

Handwriting: Variable. Usually perfectionistic in female. Often slurred or bold illegible scrawl in males. Sometimes bold flourishes or messy corrections.

Color preference: Conservative, even drab color choices: Muted colors, blue, dark or white. Aversion to red, bright colors and multicolors.

NPA type

"Sanguine-perfectionistic-aggressive type"

NPA types tend to be sanguine-complexioned, overbearing maternalistic or paternalistic extroverts. All three of the NPA traits are present and fully expressed. Exhibitionism and overt narcissism may be tempered by the P trait. The voice is LOUD and the eye contact intense. NPA types tend to be conventional in their dress and behavior. Their greatest vulnerability is the tendency to explosive rages, often followed by forced affability or apologetics. The female is sometimes denigrated as being "masculine".

Rage: Narcissistic "N rage", or aggressive "A rage" or combined "NPA rage".

Also known as: "Narcissistic-perfectionistic-aggressive type". Explosive personality. Managerial-autocratic personality. "The overbearing achiever". The sanguine autocratic tyrant.

Complexion: Tending toward sanguine or flushed in individuals of light skin color, especially when agitated.

Smile: Warm paternalistic or maternalistic smile.

Photograph: Looks at camera. Relaxed smile.

Voice: Very loud, intense, modulated. Non-stop garrulous. Pontificating.

Gestures: Active or hyperactive gestures. Intense eye contact with loud voice. Often non-seductive body contact in casual social situations.

Handwriting: Variable. Often perfectionistic but sometimes illegible.

Color preference: Rather conservative in color choice, as opposed to the more flamboyant color choices of the NA type.

Physical stature in the A and NP types

In the profiles above, trends in physical stature were noted especially in the A type and in the NP type.

The *A type* is a non-sanguine individual most prevalent in the Middle East and in Eastern Europe [6]. Short stature was noted to be frequent in this type [7].

The *NP type* is a sanguine individual, especially prevalent in parts of Western Europe [6]. Tall stature was noted to be frequent in this type in some subpopulations, but clearly not in all.

4

Inheritance of the NPA Traits

In order to be able to apply the NPA model to the problem at hand, one needs to understand a few basic concepts of genetics. In particular, one needs to appreciate the definitions of *phenotype* and *genotype*, and the difference between *dominance* and *recessiveness* in the transmission of a trait from parents to offspring. A review of some of the terminology and concepts is included in the Glossary.

On the basis of typical family pedigrees, we posited that the NPA traits are inherited according to the mechanisms of classical genetics [*8*]. In particular, the three traits:

1) obey the rule of independent assortment, and

2) follow an autosomal mechanism of transmission, with traits N and A being recessive, and P being dominant.

In simple terms, this means that the NPA traits obey the traditional laws of Mendelian genetics, with the genes underlying the traits being neither chromosomally linked together, nor sex-linked.

The possible combinations of genes ("genotypes") consistent with the various NPA types ("phenotypes") are shown overleaf in Table 1. The phenotypes listed are the Dominant types of the model, corresponding to full expression of the three NPA traits.

The recessive alleles of the N and A traits are denoted by **n** and **a,** while the dominant allele of the P trait is denoted by the capital letter **P**.

Table 1

Genotypes of the Dominant NPA types

Phenotype	*Genotype*
N	**(nn) (nna)**
A	**(aa) (naa)**
NA	**(nnaa)**
NP	**(nnP) (nnPP) (nnPa) (nnPPa)**
PA	**(Paa) (PPaa) (nPaa) (nPPaa)**
NPA	**(nnPaa) (nnPPaa)**

Table 1 shows that an individual of a particular NPA type could have one of several possible genotypes. For example, the N type has two possibilities for its underlying genotype, namely (**nn**) and (**nna**), depending on whether or not the individual is a silent carrier of the recessive **a** allele. In contrast, the NP type has four possibilities, depending, in addition, whether the dominant P allele is present in the homozygous or heterozygous state.

The NA type has only one possible genotype, the fully homozygous (**nnaa**).

Possible offspring of Dominant NPA types

For convenience, we have tabulated the possible NPA types of the offspring according to the NPA types of the parents. Allowing for all possible genotypes in the parents, we present in Table 2 the possible NPA types in the children. To read the table, one locates the NPA types of the father and mother on the horizontal and vertical axes, with the area of intersection displaying the possible NPA types in the offspring. For example, one can see that in a parental mating of NA×NP, the children could be only of the four types: N, NP, NA or NPA.

One can see from Table 2 that the restrictions on the possible NPA types of the offspring vary markedly according to the types of the parents.

	N	A	NP	NA	PA	NPA
N	N NA	"	"	"	"	"
A	N NA A	NA A	"	"	"	"
NP	N NP NA NPA	N NP NA NPA PA A	N NP NA NPA	"	"	"
NA	N NA	NA A	N NP NA NPA	NA	"	"
PA	N NP NA NPA PA A	NA NPA PA A	N NP NA NPA PA A	NA NPA PA A	NA NPA PA A	"
NPA	N NP NA NPA	NA NPA PA A	N NP NA NPA	NA NPA	NA NPA PA A	NA NPA
FATHER OR MOTHER	N	A	NP	NA	PA	NPA

Table 2. Dominant types: Possible NPA types in offspring according to the types of the parents (father or mother on either axis).

Table 2 is a simplified representation of the mechanisms of inheritance inherent in the model. Namely, it is restricted to Dominant types and neglects NPA types in whom the traits A or N may be incompletely expressed. However, neglecting this complexity of the NPA model does not interfere with our analysis of physical stature in families [9].

Non-viable types and infertility

In addition to the six possible NPA types in the offspring shown in Table 2, the model generates two other phenotypes that are unlike any of the parental types. These are the P and 0 (null) "non-viable types", as shown in Table 3 below. We recognize these types as being "non-viable" because they lack expression of either the N or A trait.

Table 3

Non-viable types in progeny

Phenotype	*Genotype*
P	(nPa) (nPPa)
0 (null)	(na)

Therefore, the model quite unexpectedly predicts *infertility* in parents of certain combinations of NPA types, namely in those couples who, because of their particular genotypes, are prone to conceive non-viable progeny of either the P or null phenotype, i.e., totally lacking both traits N and A. We presume that a fetus lacking expression of both of these traits would not survive intrauterine life, appearing as a miscarriage or stillbirth, or would "fail to thrive" in early infancy.

From the genotypes given in Tables 1 and 3, it can be shown that such infertility could occur only *in the mating of a non-aggressive type with a non-sanguine type*, namely N×A, N×PA, NP×A and NP×PA. Depending on the exact genotypes of the parents, infertility on this basis could be partial or complete [*10*].

If we update Table 2 to include the possible non-viable P and null types in the offspring, the result is Table 4 (hereafter called "the Table").

General rules pertaining to the Table

On the basis of the NPA model, with the P trait being Mendelian dominant and the N and A traits being recessive, we can state the following general rules:

- If both parents have the N trait, then all children must also have the N trait. That is, if both parents are "sanguine", all children must be sanguine.

- If both parents have the A trait, then all children must also have the A trait. That is, if both parents are "aggressive", all children must be aggressive.

- If both parents lack the P trait, then all children must also lack the P trait. That is, if both parents are "non-perfectionistic", all children must be non-perfectionistic.

	N	A	NP	NA	PA	NPA
N	N NA	"	"	"	"	"
A	N NA 0 A	NA A	"	"	"	"
NP	N NP NA NPA	N NP P NA NPA PA 0 A	N NP NA NPA	"	"	"
NA	N NA	NA A	N NP NA NPA	NA	"	"
PA	N NP P NA NPA PA 0 A	NA NPA PA A	N NP P NA NPA PA 0 A	NA NPA PA A	NA NPA PA A	"
NPA	N NP NA NPA	NA NPA PA A	N NP NA NPA	NA NPA	NA NPA PA A	NA NPA
FATHER OR MOTHER	N	A	NP	NA	PA	NPA

Table 4. Possible NPA types in offspring, including the non-viable P and 0 (null) types. Encircled are possible offspring of the four parental matches that could conceive non-viable types. These marches are: N×A, N×PA, NP×A and NP×PA.

Or conversely, the rules are:

- A non-sanguine child (who lacks the N trait) must have a parent who is also non-sanguine.

- A non-aggressive child (who lacks the A trait) must have a parent who is also non-aggressive.

- A perfectionistic child (who has the P trait) must have a parent who is also perfectionistic.

With regard to infertility, the rules are:

- Non-viable progeny can occur only if one parent is a non-sanguine type and the other is non-aggressive type.

- Neither the NA type nor the NPA type can be the parent of a non-viable type.

With regard to the "silent" carrier state:

- If a sanguine child has a non-sanguine parent, the parent must be a carrier of the recessive allele **n**.

- If an aggressive child has a non-aggressive parent, the parent must be a carrier of the recessive allele **a**.

- If a non-sanguine child has a sanguine parent, the child must be a carrier of the recessive allele **n**.

- If a non-aggressive child has an aggressive parent, the child must be a carrier of the recessive allele **a**.

Some additional conditions are:

- Parents can have children of their own NPA type, but a child's NPA type is not always the same as either parent.

- The NA type can arise in the progeny of any two parental phenotypes.

- The Table assumes no specific knowledge of the genotypes in the parents. In a specific case, where the genotypes of the parents are known, or postulated, the possibilities of the NPA types of the offspring may be more limited than those shown in the Table.

When the child is an NP type

We focus here on the NP type, in anticipation that children of this type will be especially relevant to our analysis of tall stature in offspring of short parents.

From Table 4 we can see that an NP child can have parents where either the mother or father, or both, are themselves NP types. That is, the parents can be N×NP, A×NP, NA×NP, PA×NP, NPA×NP or NP×NP. However, there are two other possibilities as well, where *neither parent is an NP type*. These are NPA×N and PA×N. It is not immediately obvious that not only these two combinations are the only possible parental matches where neither parent is an NP type but, in addition, *all the children could be NP types*. We shall return to this salient point in Chap. 6.

5

Typing People

Identifying the various NPA types

As yet, there exist no objective genetic or laboratory tests for identification of the NPA traits in an individual. The best that we can do, for the time being, is to use approximate, sometimes subjective methods.

In medicine, and especially in the areas of human behavior and psychiatry, diagnoses are frequently made on subjective criteria, typically on the basis of the diagnostic opinions of physicians. One day, all medical and psychological diagnoses will be made on the basis of laboratory tests, but we are still decades from that idealized state of affairs.

There are, nevertheless, several ways by which we can assess a person's NPA type. The ones that we consider below are: 1) by identifying specific NPA traits, 2) by *gestalt,* 3) from descriptions of an individual's appearance and behavior, 4) by identifying the N and A rages, 5) by a questionnaire, and 6) by inference from the assessed NPA types of an individual's relatives.

1. Presence of the three traits — Sometimes one can easily identify a specific trait in an individual by direct observation. For example, if one observed a child obsessively arranging toys into orderly, symmetrical arrangements, one could presume that she had the P trait.

2. An individual's gestalt — By *gestalt* we mean the general impression that an individual gives in social situations, in all of the nuances of his or her physical appearance and behavior. As we observed in the preparation of "character profiles" of the various NPA types, sometimes an individual's pattern of behavior is so distinctive that it can be easily caricaturized. Hence, we can often identify the NPA type of an individual by *gestalt* alone, just as a zoologist immediately identifies a chimpanzee without focusing on any particular physical or behavioral qualities of the animal. We can identify a particular type, say an NPA dominant type, in one fell swoop — all three traits at once — without our focusing on any particular aspect of any of the NPA traits.

3. Descriptions of an individual's appearance and behavior — An individual's NPA type, perhaps of someone long deceased, can also be assessed from written descriptions of behavior and from other archival information. If family lore has it that one's great-grandfather convincingly fit a certain pattern, then one could propose a definite NPA type for him. For example, if he were to be described as an affable gentleman with a ruddy complexion who was a vaudeville performer, and an old photograph shows him in a flowered shirt with a broad, gingival smile, then one's conjecture might be that he was an N type.

4. The N and A rages — The N or A rages may occur infrequently in a given individual, but when they do, they are typically distinctive. For example, the pallid-faced A rage in an individual of light skin color can be diagnostic of a non-sanguine A or PA type, while the vociferous, florid combined NA rage in a sanguine "managerial-autocratic" individual can be characteristic of a Dominant NPA type.

5. A questionnaire — Questionnaires or "personality tests" are often used in behavioral research in the absence of more scientific testing. Their limitations are well known, as there are a myriad of reasons why individuals might answer the various questions in different ways. Nevertheless, although personality questionnaires are not hard science, the results can certainly be used to generate hypotheses that could be tested and verified by other independent means, especially in the context of a family where individuals are genetically related.

We have available an online "NPA personality test" that is geared specifically to identify an individual's NPA type. The test can be used in two different ways. First, an individual can take the test directly to obtain results for his or her own NPA diagnosis. Second, the test can be used in a "surrogate" manner. That is, one can get an idea of another person's NPA type by taking the test "in their place," i.e., answering the questions like one thinks that he or she would answer them. Of course, one would need to know the individual very well. By this method one could even obtain an estimate of the NPA type of an individual who is long deceased, as in the case of a parent taking a "surrogate test" for a grandparent who is no longer alive.

6. *By inference from the NPA types of relatives* — Sometimes the model itself can assist in advancing a hypothetical or confirmatory diagnosis of an individual's NPA traits or type. For example, if it is unequivocal that both of a child's parents are sanguine, one can conjecture that the child — sight unseen — likewise has the N trait.

How accurate can NPA typing be?

There are several categories of ways by which the typing of an individual may be problematic:

The NPA model itself — The premise of our method of analyzing the heritability of personality is that the NPA model is basically correct. However, in the field of genetics complicating factors often present themselves in what are called *polygenic inheritance* and *genetic heterogeneity*. In simple terms, this means that 1) there may be several genes, rather than just a single one, underlying a trait, and 2) a trait caused by genes in one family can be mimicked by a different set of genes in another family. As yet, we do not have evidence that such possible complications are relevant to the NPA model, but we should be aware of this possibility.

Biological variability — As we emphasized in Chapter 2, although an individual may be distinctly male or female, or of a particular discrete NPA type, every individual has an overlay of behavioral complexity in the categories of "other genes" and environment. Although it is almost always easy to identify a person's gender, it may require some investigation — and sometimes sleuthing — to acquire enough relevant information to establish an NPA diagnosis to a degree of certainty.

Typing individuals in a particular family — The ease with which one can type individuals will necessarily vary from family to family, depending on how many individuals there are, on their NPA diagnoses, how they are related, the amount and quality of information that exists with regard to their physical appearance and behavior, and finally, on how much experience the investigating individual has had in using the NPA model.

6

Case Studies & the Solution to the Puzzle

We focus on the issue at hand: given what we have observed in the way of personality and physical stature in various families, how can we explain the existence of certain families where the parents are both of short or normal stature, while multiple children are all tall?

While such families are unusual, they are not extremely rare, either. To the question, posted recently on an internet forum, "Can short parents have tall children?" one correspondent wrote:

> *"I see it every day. My Mom is 5'7"ish, Dad is 5'8". I'm 6'3". My sister is 5'11". And it's looking like my younger sister is gonna be super tall too, like 6'4"ish."*

Our approach here will be to present a few illustrative case studies based on our experience, and with a bit of inductive reasoning see if we can arrive at a hypothesis that explains our observations. We shall keep in mind "Occam's Razor", the well-known philosophical principle that states "Don't make things more complicated than they need be." Indeed, the solution to our puzzle should straightforward and clear, so that it would be testable without equivocation.

	N	A	NP	NA	PA	NPA
N	N -- -- NA -- -- -- -- --	"	"	"	"	"
A	N -- -- NA -- -- 0 A	-- -- -- NA -- -- -- A	"	"	"	"
NP	N NP -- NA NPA -- -- --	N NP P NA NPA PA 0 A	N NP -- NA NPA -- -- --	"	"	"
NA	N -- -- NA -- -- -- --	-- -- -- NA -- -- -- A	N NP -- NA NPA -- -- --	-- -- -- NA -- -- -- --	"	"
PA	N NP P NA NPA PA 0 A	-- -- -- NA NPA PA -- A	N NP P NA NPA PA 0 A	-- -- -- NA NPA PA -- A	-- -- -- NA NPA PA -- A	"
NPA	N NP -- NA NPA -- -- --	-- -- -- NA NPA PA -- A	N NP -- NA NPA -- -- --	-- -- -- NA NPA -- -- --	-- -- -- NA NPA PA -- A	-- -- -- NA NPA -- -- --
FATHER OR MOTHER	N	A	NP	NA	PA	NPA

Table 5. "The Table": Possible NPA types in offspring according to the NPA types of the parents. Shown encircled are the possible types of the offspring for the parental matches NPA×N and PA×N on the assumption that the parental genotypes are unknown.

"The Table"

We shall use for our analyses the table that we derived previously for "Possible NPA phenotypes in offspring." For convenience, it is reproduced above as Table 5. The Table displays for Dominant types all possible types of the offspring on the assumption that the parental genotypes are unknown. If the genotypes are known (or postulated), then it may be possible to eliminate some of the possibilities in the NPA types of the offspring.

In the Table, the parental matches NPA×N and PA×N are encircled. *These are the only possible parental combinations where neither parent is an NP type, but all of the children — no matter how many — could be NP types.*

Case examples

Case 1. Sylvester, an auctioneer by profession, is a dynamic individual of the NPA Dominant type. His wife, Wendy, runs a children's day care center and is an N type. Sylvester and Wendy are both of average height. They have two sons and three daughters, all of whom are very tall (above 6 ft 2 in, or 188 cm). In contrast to the personality types of their parents, all of the children are NP types. Both the paternal and maternal grandparents are not particularly tall. Wendy has had no miscarriages, and they have not had any issues of infertility. What could be going on here?

From the Table it can be seen that, allowing for all possible genotypes in the parents, the children of a NPA×N parental match could be N, NP, NA or NPA types, with no predicted problems of infertility. But the children in the case example are all NP types. How could this happen?

This could occur only if 1) Sylvester is homozygous for the P trait, and 2) Wendy is not a carrier of the recessive **a** allele of the A trait. Thus, the genotypes of the parents must be Sylvester: (**nnPPaa**) and Wendy: (**nn**), and it follows that all of the children would be NP types of genotype (**nnPa**). Thus, all of the children are silent carriers of the recessive **a** allele, but they do not have the phenotypic A trait.

Furthermore, since Sylvester is homozygous for the dominant P trait, this means that both of his parents must have had the P trait, as well. Similarly, since Wendy is not a carrier of the A trait, this means that neither of her parents had the A trait. They must have been either N or NP types.

This is an example of how analysis of *phenotypes* in related individuals can allow one to determine their *genotypes*.

Now, we come to the interesting information that the NP children are all very tall. Is it just a strange coincidence that all of the children are NP types and also are tall, while their parents are not NP types and not tall? Given that we have frequently observed NP types to be of tall stature in some general populations, we should consider the possibility that the NP personality type and stature are somehow linked in this family.

Case 2. Amanda, a trial lawyer, is clearly an energetic NPA Dominant type. Her husband, Luke, is an actor in daytime drama shows and is an N type. They are both of average height. They have a son and three daughters. The children all have different NPA types: the son is an NA type, while the daughters' types are N, NP and NPA. All of the children are of average or slightly above average height, except the NP daughter, who is 6 ft 4 in! How could this happen?

From the Table, it can be seen that an NPA×N parental match can indeed have offspring of N, NA, NP and NPA types, so that is evidently what happened here. In order for this to occur, the parental genotypes must be Amanda: (**nnPaa**) and Luke: (**nna**). That is, Amanda must be heterozygous for the P trait, while Luke must be a carrier of the recessive allele **a**. It can be shown that all of the above NPA types in the children should theoretically occur with equal probability.

What is interesting, of course, is that only the NP daughter is tall. Again, is it just a coincidence that only the NP daughter is tall, while her parents and siblings — who are not NP types — are of normal stature? Once more, we are drawn to propose that there might be a link between the sudden appearance of a NP type and the sudden appearance of tall stature in this family.

In the above two cases, the issue of possible infertility did not occur, as it can be seen that the parental match NPA×N is not prone to non-viable types in the offspring (miscarriage, etc.).

Case 3. Yevgeny is a systems analyst employed in the Kremlin and is a PA type. His wife, Ludmila, is a costume designer with the Bolshoi Academy and is an N type. They have four children, all NP types, but Ludmila has had many miscarriages and one stillbirth. Yevgeny and Ludmila are both of average height, but the four children are all above 6 ft 2 in! How could this happen?

From the Table we can see that, allowing for all possible genotypes in the parents, the children of a PA×N parental match could be any of the Dominant types: N, NP, NA, NPA, PA or A. In addition, the non-viable P and null types are possible, so this type of union is prone to problems of infertility. But in the example, the children are all NP types. How could this happen?

As in Case 1, this can occur only if 1) Yevgeny is homozygous for the P trait, and 2) Ludmila is not a carrier of the recessive **a** allele of the A trait. Thus, the genotypes of the parents must be Yevgeny: (**nPPaa**) and Wendy: (**nn**), and it follows that all of the viable children must be NP types of genotype (**nnPa**). Once again, all of the children are silent carriers of the recessive **a** allele, but they do not have the phenotypic A trait.

This union is prone to infertility, as it can be shown that 50 percent of conceptions would theoretically be P or null types (genotypes **nPa** or **na**). In general, infertility will arise in matches where one parent is a non-sanguine type and the other is a non-aggressive type.

Once again, we have here a family in which neither parent is an NP type, but all of the viable children are NP types. And, once again, it is only the NP members of the family who are tall.

Case 4. Feliks is an Estonian sea captain of the PA type who marries Natia, a Polynesian lady of the N type. Neither Feliks nor Natia is tall. They have three children of types PA, N and NA, all of whom are of normal stature. After the tragic death of Natia, Feliks marries her identical twin sister, Talia, by whom he soon has an NP daughter who is much taller than either parent. Both sisters had several miscarriages. How can we explain this family?

From the Table it can be seen that the viable offspring of a parental match PA×N can be any one of the six Dominant types. Since some of Natia's children lack the P trait but have the A trait, this means that Feliks must be heterozygous for the P trait and Natia must have been a carrier of the A trait. Thus, the genotypes of the parents must be Feliks: (**nPaa**) and Natia: (**nna**). Talia is genetically identical to her sister, so the fact that an NP child did not previously appear among her sister's children was just a matter of chance. It can be shown that all six of the Dominant types are equally probable in this family, and that the risk of non-viable pregnancy (P or null type) is 25 percent.

Once again, the appearance of a tall individual of the NP type in a family where no one else is of this type raises the issue of a genetic link between the personality type and physical stature.

Evaluation

Correlation of NP type with physical stature

Our aim is to propose the simplest genetic mechanism consistent with our observations. The issue that needs to be addressed is whether the apparent correlation between NP type and tall physical stature is a real one, and whether it rests on a logical genetic mechanism.

Given the polymorphic nature of Western society, our observations of a high prevalence of tall NP types in the *general population* could be dismissed as being subjective, unmethodical and uncontrolled. However, given that we have observed *families* in which the only tall individuals were NP types, makes it more likely that the correlation is a real one.

The case of non-NP parents with NP children

Our illustrative examples focused on the special situation where the parents of NP children were not NP types themselves. The parental matches where this could occur were only of two kinds: NPA×N and PA×N. Sometimes, consistent with NPA genetics, *all* of the children were NP types, as if they were hybrids of two different parental types.

The clue to the solution of our puzzle is the special case of the parental match NPA×N. How does the NP type of the child differ genetically from the parents? It is not because of the N trait because both of the parents, as well as the child, have this trait. In fact, the differences between the parents and child are 1) the P trait is present in the child and only one of the parents, and 2) the absence of A trait is present in the child and the other parent. Thus, the appearance of the NP type in this parental match is due to *two dominant genes, one being inherited from the mother and one from the father.*

Consider the case of the parental match NPA×N, where the father is NPA type and the mother is N type. In the NP child, the child receives the *P trait* only from the father (dominant gene **P**) and *lack of A trait* only from the mother (dominant gene **A₀**). Note that since the A trait is recessive, its converse, lack of A trait, is regulated by a dominant allele. In short, the genes **P** and **A₀** act as a pair of *complementary genes* to produce the NP phenotype that is different from either parent.

The case where *all* the children are NP types

In parental matches of the kind NPA×N, sometimes all of the children are NP types, as in Case 1. This occurs when the NPA parent is homozygous for the P trait (genotype **PP**) and the N parent is homozygous for lack of the A trait (genotype **A₀A₀**).

Similarly, in parental matches of the kind PA×N, sometimes all of the viable children are NP types, as in Case 3. Once again, this occurs when the PA parent is homozygous for the P trait (genotype **PP**) and the N parent is homozygous for lack of the A trait (genotype **A₀A₀**). However, this PA×N match is subject to infertility (P and null progeny), so that the result of any pregnancy is either a viable NP child or a non-viable fetus that does not survive to maturity.

The solution to the puzzle: Complementary genes

Our puzzle: How is it that parents who are both of short stature can have multiple children who are tall?

The simplest solution is as follows. Just as genes **P** and **A₀** can act as complementary genes to produce the NP phenotype in matches where neither parent is an NP type, the *same genes* can produce tall stature when present together. Thus, in our case examples, neither the N parent nor the matched NPA or PA parent is of tall stature because each has only <u>one</u> of the genes (**P** or **A₀**) expressed. Each gene in itself evidently has only a modest influence on stature. It takes the expression of both genes acting synergistically together to produce a large effect on physical stature. Apparently, this effect on stature of only two genes can be enormous in some families.

So, our solution in a nutshell is:

The phenomenon of multiple tall children in parents who are of short or normal stature can be the result of a single pair of pleiotropic dominant complementary genes. The two genes are inherited, one from each parent, and have a large synergistic effect on physical stature when present together. The two genes likewise code for personality traits, namely perfectionism and inhibition of aggression, providing a link between personality traits and body physique.

If each of the two genes is present in the homozygous state in the parents, then all of the children would necessarily inherit the pair of complementary genes. In this case, all of the children would tend to be of tall stature and also have the characteristic personality traits of perfectionism and inhibition of aggression.

Or, the solution in plainer language:

A particular pair of short parents can have tall children when the children receive two interacting genes, one from each parent. The two genes each have only a minimal effect on height when present alone in the parents, but when brought together in the children as "complementary genes", the effect can be dramatic. The same two genes code for the personality traits of perfectionism and inhibition of aggression, demonstrating a link between personality traits and body physique.

If each of the two genes is present in the homozygous state in the parents, then all of the children of this parental match — no matter how many — would inherit the two genes. In this case, all of the children would tend to be tall and all would have the sanguine NP personality type characteristic of perfectionism and lack of aggression.

7

Conclusion

The hurdles of conventional wisdom

The NPA model of personality, being based on three traits, each of which is dependent on the expression of a single gene, is a bit out of step with current thinking. Indeed, the conventional wisdom of the day is that personality traits are highly heritable, but because of genetic heterogeneity and the polygenic nature of personality traits, no single gene contributes more than a few percent to the total effect on any aspect of human behavior [*11*].

Our model implies that this particular bit of conventional wisdom is wrong. If, for example, the observed trait of perfectionism were the result of many genes, then it would not be frequently transmitted from a parent to a child. But we know that this is not true: very frequently a child diagnosed with autism or with an obsessive-compulsive personality disorder will have one parent having the same constrained personality type (the NP type of our model).

With regard to the genetic basis of physical stature, the situation is similar. The conventional wisdom is that with so many genes possibly affecting a person's stature, there can be no single gene causing an effect more than a few percent, this way or that.

Why, then, have researchers not found a pair of genes that — according to our analysis — can have dramatic effects on physical stature in certain families? The answer most likely is that the relevant genes are *complementary genes* that act in concert. They are not likely to be detected in "genome wide" searches of diverse populations where they often occur separately or are overwhelmed by other genes that affect stature.

The implication is that potential progress in this field lies in the realm of family studies, rather than in unsystematic "genome-wide" searches for genes affecting physical stature.

Summary

- The problem at hand is to solve the enigma of how parents of short or normal stature can have multiple children who are all tall.

- The basis of our analysis is a model of personality based on three genetic traits: sanguinity (N), perfectionism (P) and aggression (A).

- The personality model produces a limited number of discrete personality types.

- One of the personality types, the NP type, is characterized by two dominant genes, corresponding to perfectionism **P** and the inhibition of aggression $\mathbf{A_0}$, thus having genotype $\mathbf{PA_0}$. This NP personality type is associated with tall stature in the absence of other genes that code for short stature.

- According to the NPA model, there can be families where neither parent is an NP type but either some of the children, or all of the children, are NP types. In such cases, one of the parents carries the gene **P** and the other parent carries the gene $\mathbf{A_0}$. Thus, the NP children in these families are the result the pair of complementary genes $\mathbf{PA_0}$, one received from each parent. Tall stature results from the pleiotropic effect of the same pair of complementary genes on physical stature, providing a link between personality type and stature.

- In these families, the parents are not tall because the dominant genes **P** and **A$_0$** by themselves have only a modest effect on physical stature. But if they are present together as a pair of complementary genes in a child, the effect on stature can be dramatic.

- There are two possible parental matches in families where neither parent is an NP type but either some of the children, or all of the children, are NP types. These are NPA×N and PA×N. These same two parental matches are the basis of some families where neither parent is tall, but some or all of the children are tall.

- The PA×N parental match is prone to problems of infertility due to the appearance of non-viable progeny (a fetus lacking both traits N and A). The NPA×N parental match has no such problems of infertility.

- Families where the parents are of short or normal stature and <u>all</u> of the children are tall occur when one parent (NPA or PA type) is homozygous for the P gene (genotype **PP**) and the other parent (N type) is homozygous for the gene corresponding to the inhibition of aggression (genotype **A$_0$A$_0$**).

- The solution to the enigma of how parents of short or normal stature can have multiple children who are all tall is: *the tall children have at least one pair of dominant, pleotropic, complementary genes, with one gene being inherited from each parent.*

APPENDIX

NPA PERSONALITY THEORY: SYNOPSIS
Personality theory based on the genetic traits of sanguinity, perfectionism and aggression

The NPA theory of personality was developed by A.M. Benis on the basis of concepts presented over fifty years ago by psychiatrist Karen Horney. The model posits three major behavioral traits underlying personality: sanguinity (N), perfectionism (P) and aggression (A), leading to the formulation of discrete character types. Each trait is based on a major pleiotropic gene (a gene determining several related characteristics) that follows the rules of Mendelian genetics.

The NPA model proposes that the character traits A and N are indispensable to human development, being related to the sympathetic and parasympathetic nervous systems, respectively. The trait P is also assumed to function at the level of the central nervous system and to act as a modifier of the expression of traits A and N. The NPA model proposes to clarify the genetic bases of known personality disorders, diseases related to behavioral factors ("psychosomatic diseases") and mental illnesses.

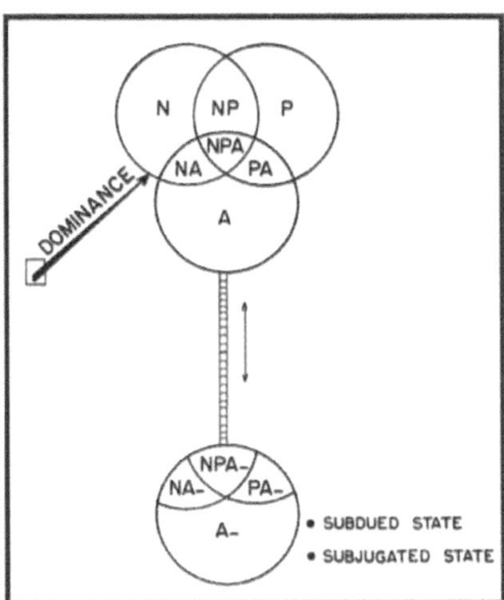

Fig. A1. Venn diagram of Dominant character types. Character types having the trait of aggression A may be reduced, reversibly, to a subdued or subjugated state A–.

Contents

- 1 What is personality?
- 2 NPA model based on three genetic traits
  - 2.1 Genetics and environment
  - 2.2 Traits of sanguinity, perfectionism and aggression
    - 2.2.1 Aggression (A)
    - 2.2.2 Sanguinity (N)
    - 2.2.3 Perfectionism (P)
- 3 Character types
  - 3.1_Dominance: Dominant types
    - 3.1.1 N type
    - 3.1.2 A type
    - 3.1.3 NA type
    - 3.1.4 NP type
    - 3.1.5 PA type
    - 3.1.6 NPA type
  - 3.2_Submission: Passive Aggressive types
    - 3.2.1 Non-compliant types
    - 3.2.2 Compliant types
  - 3.3_Resignation: Resigned types
- 4 Borderline types and mental illness
- 5 Dominance and submission
- 6 Mendelian transmission of NPA traits
- 7 Implications of a trait theory based on genetics
  - 7.1 Population Genetics
  - 7.2 Evolutionary origins of NPA traits
  - 7.3 Predictive aspects of NPA model
- 8 Criticism and controversy
- 9 References
- 10 Citations
- 11 Illustrations
- 12_Source

What is personality?

Psychologists speak of personality as "a collection of emotional, thought and behavioral patterns unique to a person that is consistent over time" [1]. Although many investigators have proposed various theories of personality, no objectively testable model has emerged. The NPA model falls into the category of a trait theory of personality, its unique approach being that it is biologically based on classical human genetics.

NPA model based on three genetic traits

Genetics and environment

Although it is universally accepted that both genetic and environmental factors (or "nature and nurture") comprise personality, the relevant genes have yet to be identified [2]. Studies of the heritability of personality factors conducted with identical and fraternal twins emphasize the importance of genetics in behavior [3]. The NPA model acknowledges the possible importance of environment and culture in personality but emphasizes that it is the genetic, or structural, factors that first need to be identified.

The NPA model acknowledges that the genetic bases of personality are themselves complex. It assumes at least four tiers to this genetic basis:

- male or female gender

- character type based on the three NPA traits

- temperament, or the degree of activity or excitability of an individual in the Pavlovian sense

- other facets of personality, such as Raymond Cattell's 16 Personality Factors or Hans Eysenck's P-E-N model of personality.

The NPA model, thus, focuses on only the second of these four tiers, acknowledging that temperament and other facets of personality may involve a large number of genes.

Fig. A2. Karen Horney (1885-1952)

Traits of sanguinity, perfectionism and aggression

Karen Horney advanced the concept that at maturity there exist at least three expansive character types, namely the "narcissistic", the "perfectionistic" and the "arrogant-vindictive" [5]. Extending these ideas, the NPA model posits that the human character rests primarily on the existence of three major traits: sanguinity (N), perfectionism (P) and aggression (A). Each of these traits is assumed to exist as the expression of a single major pleiotropic gene. Horney considered that the traits have environmental origins, being the result of an individual's desperate search for dominance in the context of a stifling upbringing [5]. The NPA model — in ascribing the traits to genetic origins — emphasizes biological attributes associated with the traits.

Aggression (A)

The behavioral trait of aggression is proposed to be the most labile of the three [6]. The stereotypic acts associated with this trait involve body posturing, gestures, and eye contact of intimidation and deference, with individuals having this trait continually competing with each other on a scale of dominance and submission. The trait of aggression corresponds to a striving for *power* over one's environment, hence it is one main component of competitiveness in social relations, or ambition. In a pejorative connotation the trait may reveal itself in the context of sadism or sadomasochism. The facial expression is non-sanguine, i.e., tending toward sallowness or pallor in individuals of light skin color. The hallmark of the trait of aggression is a mass discharge of the sympathetic nervous system: the "flight or fight" response or the aggressive-vindictive rage. During the expression of this rage, the facial complexion of pallor is accentuated.

Sanguinity (N)

The trait of sanguinity (Horney's "narcissism") is proposed to be less labile than that of aggression (where individuals may be constantly altering their character states on a scale of dominance and submission) [6]. The stereotypic acts associated with the trait include self-flaunting body posturing, expansive arm gestures, bowing, instinctive self-adornment, and a natural attraction to the limelight of personal recognition. Individuals having only this trait (of the three) are competitive but non-aggressive in their strivings for recognition. The trait corresponds to a striving for *glory* in one's environment, representing the second main component of human ambition. In the absence of mediating factors, the unbridled trait of sanguinity may reveal itself in the context of conceit, exhibitionism, vanity or messianism. An associated facial expression includes the radiant gingival smile (broadly exposing the gums and teeth). The facial complexion in individuals of light skin color tends toward blood-red or ruddy. Hallmarks of the trait include blushing, flushing, and a mass discharge of the autonomic nervous system: the narcissistic rage of defense and withdrawal. During expression of this rage the normally sanguine complexion becomes even more florid.

Perfectionism (P)

The trait of perfectionism in the NPA model is not a basic drive of ambition and is not associated with a rage reaction [6]. Rather it is a mediator of the unbridled drives of aggression and/or sanguinity. The stereotypic acts associated with the trait of perfectionism are obsessiveness, compulsiveness, repetition, and the maintenance of neatness, order and symmetry. A clue to the nature of the trait lies in the compulsive, repetitive mannerisms of autistic children and some adult schizophrenic individuals. The behavioral pattern is often ritualistic and the speech characterized by echolalia. It is posited that such autistic and schizophrenic individuals are those in whom the two components of ambition, i.e., aggression and sanguinity, have been suppressed by genetic or environmental factors, either congenitally, in childhood, or after maturity, thus revealing in the individual a primitive state of perfectionism.

Character types

The notion that humans exhibit only a limited number of discrete character types can be traced back to the time of the ancient Greeks, in particular to the theory of humors (blood, black bile, yellow bile and phlegm). The NPA model attempts to relate genetic NPA types to these character types of antiquity, as well as to the classic personality disorders of modern psychiatry.

Fig. A3. Character types according to the ancient theory of humors: *Phlegmaticus, Cholericus, Sanguineus* and *Melancholicus.* [*J.K. Lavater, ca. 1775*]

Dominance: Dominant character types

In Dominant types the traits A and N, if present at all, are fully expressed [6]. The NPA model generates the following character types:

N type

The *sanguine (N) type* is found in the writings of Horney [7] and others who have developed the classic psychiatric views of narcissism. In the NPA model this type is the equivalent of the sanguine character type described by the ancients. The important attributes of this type are: expansiveness but unaggressiveness, non-perfectionism, a tendency to flamboyant self-adornment, a natural attraction to the limelight, the gingival smile of recognition and the florid narcissistic rage. In extreme forms this type appears as a self-anointed visionary, a proselytizing evangelist or a messianic personality.

A type

The *aggressive (A) type* corresponds to Horney's arrogant-vindictive type and to her concept of "moving against people" [8]. In the NPA model this is the classic choleric character type of antiquity. The main attributes of this type are: unbridled arrogance, instinctual vindictiveness, non-perfectionism, no tendency to self-adornment, a wry or sardonic grin in place of a gingival smile, and the pallid-complexioned aggressive-vindictive rage. In extreme forms this type appears as a sadistic personality, as an extroverted paranoid personality, or as the so-called antisocial or sociopathic personality.

NA type

The *sanguine-aggressive (NA) type* is regarded to be a composite of the previously described sanguine and aggressive types. Horney described the essence of this character type, in the female, in an article, "The overvaluation of love: a study of a common present day type" [9]. The main attributes of this type are: a sanguine complexion, synergistic merging of unbridled narcissism and aggression, hyperactivity, non-perfectionism, a tendency toward extreme self-adornment, exhibitionism in the limelight, a "flashy" extroverted smile and a tendency toward aggressive-vindictive or combined narcissistic-aggressive rages. In extreme forms this type appears as the hypomanic, histrionic or hysterical personality.

NP type

The attributes of the *sanguine-perfectionist (NP) type* were described by Horney in her exposition of the "perfectionist type" [4]. In the NPA model this encompasses the classic phlegmatic type known to the ancients. The main qualities of this type are: a tendency toward a sanguine complexion, industriousness, orderliness, an intense sense of duty, unaggressiveness, stubbornness, negativism, a tendency to ruminate, perfectionistic rather than unbridled self-adornment, an uncommonly seen gingival smile of recognition, and the capacity to exhibit the florid narcissistic rage. In extreme forms this character appears as the obsessive-compulsive personality.

PA type

The *perfectionistic-aggressive (PA)* type is alluded to by Horney in her mention of aggressive types who function in the capacity of a "power behind the throne" [8], that is, personages who utilize intellectual qualities and planning rather than overt aggression to achieve their aims. In the NPA model this is the classic non-sanguine, austere melancholic personality of the ancients. The principal qualities of this type are: a non-sanguine complexion, passive-aggressive behavior, dour perfectionism, vigilance, manipulativeness, a proud bearing, haughty reservedness, a calculated vindictiveness, a lack of an innate tendency to self-adornment, a sardonic grin, and the pallid aggressive-vindictive rage. In extreme forms this is the passive-aggressive, rebellious-distrustful, or ruminating paranoid personality.

NPA type

The *sanguine-perfectionistic-aggressive (NPA) type* was not explicitly described by Horney, although she did note that the three traits can coexist in the same individual [10]. The main attributes of this type are: a sanguine complexion, a loud voice, dynamism with a tendency to be overbearing, bombastic garrulity, intense eye contact, a strong sense of duty, a bent toward conventional values, unpretentious self-adornment, an outgoing smile of moderate intensity, and the capacity to exhibit the narcissistic, aggressive, or explosive narcissistic-aggressive rages. In the extreme cases this individual is the managerial-autocratic or explosive personality.

Submission: Passive Aggressive character types

In Passive Aggressive types the trait of aggression is not fully expressed [6]. The NPA model defines two gradations of relative submission: *non-compliance*, in which the individual is basically submissive but is easily activated to an energetic state of aggression, and *compliance*, in which the individual tends to remain in a profound state of submission.

In the model the state of submission, or inhibition of aggression, most often has a genetic basis, the result of a congenital, incomplete expression of the gene for the trait A. However, the model also allows for environmental causes, the state of submission being induced during the juvenile period on the basis of environmental constraints to character development. That is, phenocopies (based on environmental factors) of a genetically disposed submissive state may exist. Also, like Dominant types having full expression of the trait A, Passive Aggressive types may exhibit the aggressive A rage.

Non-compliant types

The model denotes the state of non-compliance by A–, obtaining the following *non-compliant* phenotypes:

- **Aggressive (A–)**
- **Perfectionistic-aggressive (PA–)**
- **Sanguine (NA–)**
- **Sanguine-perfectionistic (NPA–)**

Compliant types

The model denotes the state of compliance by A=, obtaining the following *compliant* phenotypes:

- **Aggressive (A=)**
- **Perfectionistic-aggressive (PA=)**
- **Sanguine (NA=)**
- **Sanguine-perfectionistic (NPA=)**

The *NPA– non-compliant type* above corresponds to active, motivated, non-confrontational individuals whose baseline personality tends toward submissiveness, as described by Horney in her discussion of "inverted sadistic" behavior [11]. In the therapeutic setting, these individuals are found over the spectrum of the "Type A", dependent, and phobic-anxious personality. The *NA– type* is a non-perfectionistic, active individual, often exhibiting unbridled narcissistic behavior. In the therapeutic setting this is a cyclothymic or dependent histrionic personality.

The *compliant types NA=* and *NPA=* above correspond to more profoundly submissive individuals, having more pronounced tendencies toward masochistic behavior [12]. They correspond to Horney's compliant "self-effacing" personality and to her concept of "moving toward people" [13].

Resignation: Resigned character types

In the character state of resignation, the trait of aggression is stunted after maturity because of environmental constraints [6]. Unlike the Passive Aggressive types who readily involve themselves in the relative competition of dominance and submission (and sometimes sadomasochism), Resigned types remain relatively detached from such activities and only with difficulty can be stressed to an A+ state of active aggression. However, like Passive Aggressive types, the Resigned types can be induced into the aggressive-vindictive A rage.

The model denotes the state of resignation by –A, obtaining the following phenotypes:

- **Aggressive (–A)**
- **Perfectionistic-aggressive (P–A)**
- **Sanguine (N–A)**
- **Sanguine-perfectionistic (NP–A)**

The sanguine Resigned types, having the N trait, correspond to detached individuals, as described by Horney. She considered that "moving away from people" was a maladaptive response that could develop as a growing individual struggled toward maturity [14]. The *NP–A type* would tend to have strong perfectionistic tendencies, while the *N–A type* would be more labile.

Borderline types and mental illness

In the NPA model *Borderline types* possess only one of the traits of ambition (N or A) and it is only partially expressed. Types in which both traits (N and A) are either absent or profoundly suppressed fall into categories of mental illness, in particular schizophrenia [6]. Thus, NPA theory predicts that the categories of Borderline personality and schizophrenia are heterogeneous, depending on the underlying NPA character structure. Examples of Borderline types would be the A– or PA– types above. Types falling into the categories of mental illness would be the compliant submissive types, A= or PA=.

One aspect of the model focuses on the Dominant types N and NP, which lack the trait A [6]. In analogy with partial expression of the trait A, the theory identifies states of incomplete expression of the trait N, denoted as N–, N= and –N. Examples of Borderline types would be N– or N– P types. Types falling into the categories of mental illness would be N= or N=P, the latter being a perfectionistic, autistic individual.

Dominance and submission

In the NPA model, Dominant character types having the trait A have the potential of being reduced to an A– subdued state acutely or to a subjugated state chronically (see Fig. A1 above). Similarly, non-compliant Passive Aggressive types have the potential of being activated to an energetic A+ state resembling dominance, usually for short periods of time. Thus, the model emphasizes the potential lability of trait A in social relations, with Dominant and Passive Aggressive types continually altering their behavior in competitive interactions with other individuals and in the context of mating. In the extreme, some of these relationships fall into the category of sadomasochism [15]. Resigned types, in their detachment from social interactions, steadfastly avoid dominance-submission relationships and, in particular, hierarchal structures where "pecking orders" predominate.

Mendelian transmission of NPA traits

On the basis of archetypal examples, the model assumes that in their full expression the NPA traits are transmitted by autosomal genes, with traits A and N being recessive and trait P being transmitted in the dominant mode [6]. The alleles corresponding to full expression and total suppression of the trait A are denoted by $\mathbf{a}$ and $\mathbf{A_0}$, respectively, and the corresponding alleles for the trait N are denoted by $\mathbf{n}$ and $\mathbf{N_0}$. For the trait P two alleles $\mathbf{P}$ and $\mathbf{p_0}$ are posited, corresponding to full expression or total absence of the trait P, on the assumption that the trait is transmitted with complete penetrance. This scheme of inheritance is consistent with the notion that the alleles $\mathbf{A_0}$ and $\mathbf{N_0}$ control the production of inhibitors of the traits A and N at the level of the central nervous system, with alleles $\mathbf{A_0}$ and $\mathbf{N_0}$ being dominant with respect to $\mathbf{a}$ and $\mathbf{n}$. The scheme leads directly to Table A1, showing the possible phenotypes of progeny according to the phenotypes of the parents:

The table shows:

- N and A individuals need not have N or A parents. Such individuals can arise *de novo* so long as at least one of the parents is an NP and PA individual, respectively.

- PA individuals must have at least one parent who is of either the PA or A type.

- NP individuals must have at least one parent who is of either the NP or N type.

- NA individuals can arise *de novo* from any combination of phenotypes.

- The mating of two NA types can yield progeny of only NA types.

- The mating of an NPA type with an NA type can yield progeny of only NPA or NA types.

- Certain combinations of parental genotypes may lead to zygotes having only the P trait (P phenotype) or lacking all three traits (null phenotype, denoted by 0). According to NPA theory, zygotes of P or null phenotype would be non-viable. Thus, the model predicts partial or complete infertility in some combinations of parental phenotypes, these being N×A, N×PA, NP×A and NP×PA.

N	N -- -- NA -- -- -- -- --	"	"	"	"	"
A	N -- -- NA -- -- 0 A	-- -- -- NA -- -- -- A	"	"	"	"
NP	N NP -- NA NPA -- -- --	N NP P NA NPA PA 0 A	N NP -- NA NPA -- -- --	"	"	"
NA	N -- -- NA -- -- -- --	-- -- -- NA -- -- -- A	N NP -- NA NPA -- -- --	-- -- -- NA -- -- -- --	"	"
PA	N NP P NA NPA PA 0 A	-- -- -- NA NPA PA -- A	N NP P NA NPA PA 0 A	-- -- -- NA NPA PA -- A	-- -- -- NA NPA PA -- A	"
NPA	N NP -- NA NPA -- -- --	-- -- -- NA NPA PA -- A	N NP -- NA NPA -- -- --	-- -- -- NA NPA -- -- --	-- -- -- NA NPA PA -- A	-- -- -- NA NPA -- -- --
FATHER OR MOTHER	N	A	NP	NA	PA	NPA

Table A1. Possible phenotypes of children according to the phenotypes of the parents. The phenotypes of the father and mother are shown along the axes of the table. The P and null (0) phenotypes by the model are non-viable and would result in miscarriage, stillbirth or an infant who fails to thrive.

Implications of a trait theory based on genetics

Population Genetics

A trait theory based on genetics would imply that the personality structure of a population could be expressed in definitive mathematical terms. The NPA model is amenable to the Hardy-Weinberg approach to quantify the distribution of NPA character types in a given subpopulation [16]. With the usual assumptions of gene frequencies n, p and a and random mating, incidences of Dominant character types are given in Table A2, below. Because of the occurrence of non-viable P and null (0) phenotypes, the assumptions of Hardy-Weinberg equilibrium would not be strictly valid: the incidences generated by the expressions in Table A2 below represent the phenotypes of the first generation only.

The assumption of numerical values for the three gene frequencies n, p and a generates a hypothetical subpopulation, or habitancy [16]. In Table A3 six habitancies are given with descriptive labels: *Polymorphic,* (or "Balanced"), *Punctilious, Sublime, Demonstrative, Authoritarian* and *Militant*. The intent of the labels is to emphasize the very different tenors of each of the distributions of character types.

The table demonstrates that:

- Relatively small changes in gene frequencies could cause large changes in the phenotype frequencies.

- The frequencies of non-viable P and null types are low for these habitancies, on the order of 0 to 8 percent.

Relative incidence of phenotypes on basis of gene frequencies *n*, *p* and *a*

Phenotype	Relative incidence
N	$n^2 \times (1\text{-}p)^2 \times (1\text{-}a^2)$
A	$(1\text{-}n^2) \times (1\text{-}p)^2 \times a^2$
NP	$n^2 \times p(2\text{-}p) \times (1\text{-}a^2)$
NA	$n^2 \times (1\text{-}p)^2 \times a^2$
PA	$(1\text{-}n^2) \times p(2\text{-}p) \times a^2$
NPA	$n^2 \times p(2\text{-}p) \times a^2$
P	$2n(1\text{-}n) \times p(2\text{-}p) \times 2a(1\text{-}a)$
null (0)	$2n(1\text{-}n) \times (1\text{-}p)^2 \times 2a(1\text{-}a)$

Table A2. Relative incidences of phenotypes for the first generation. The incidence for each phenotype is the product of three probabilities, corresponding to the presence or absence of the three traits N, P and A. The P and null types are non-viable and contribute neither to parentage nor issue.

HABITANCY

Phenotype	Balanced	Punctilious	Sublime	Demonstrative	Authoritarian	Militant
N	7	3	77	2	1	1
A	3	<1	<1	2	17	34
NP	22	78	18	7	2	1
NA	13	<1	3	20	6	11
PA	9	2	<1	7	52	35
NPA	39	8	1	61	17	12
P	4	8	<1	1	4	2
null (0)	1	<1	1	<1	1	2
Gene frequencies	$n = 0.90$ $p = 0.50$ $a = 0.80$	$n = 0.90$ $p = 0.80$ $a = 0.30$	$n = 0.99$ $p = 0.10$ $a = 0.20$	$n = 0.95$ $p = 0.50$ $a = 0.95$	$n = 0.50$ $p = 0.50$ $a = 0.95$	$n = 0.50$ $p = 0.30$ $a = 0.95$

Table A3. Frequencies of phenotypes in six habitancies (per 100 zygotes, or pregnancies). The P and null (0) phenotypes are non-viable. Non-viable types arise when the zygote has neither trait N nor A. The above analysis is confined to Dominant character types on the assumption of two alleles for each NPA gene.

Evolutionary origins of NPA traits

The assumption of a genetic basis for the traits N, P and A implies that their origins reside in the evolution of humans from precursor species, and in particular, that the traits are likely to be found in primates other than *Homo sapiens*. As examples, the model leads to proposed character types as follows:

- The omnivorous, hierarchal, unsmiling olive baboon, known for its lengthy grooming rituals, would be a likely perfectionist-aggressive PA type.

- The herbivorous, aloof, phlegmatic orangutan and gorilla, capable of gingival smiles, would be likely NP types.

- Akin to humans, the omnivorous, promiscuous chimpanzee, also capable of the gingival smile, would likely have a heterogeneous distribution of types, with NA and NPA types predominating.

Fig. A4. NPA theory proposes that the olive baboon is a likely perfectionist-aggressive PA type.

Predictive aspects of NPA model

The model would have the potential to be predictive in the following categories:

- The possible genetic character types of children could be deduced from the character types of parents.

- Relations could be defined between genetic character type and susceptibility to certain physical and mental diseases.

- Combinations of parental character types prone to infertility problems (miscarriage and stillbirth) could be identified, these combinations being ones which permit the occurrence of a fetus having neither trait N nor A.

- Allele frequencies for the NPA traits, as well as the resultant distributions of NPA character types, in various societies could be analyzed on the basis of well-known principles of population genetics.

- Studies with primates could confirm a biological basis for behavior in the areas of sociobiology and evolutionary psychology.

Criticism and controversy

Controversy has always followed past positions taken by the scientific community relating human behavior to inheritance, as in Arthur Jensen's theories of intelligence, Herrnstein and Murray's "The Bell Curve", or Lewontin and colleagues' "Not in Our Genes". The NPA personality theory is not exempt. The result of the "nature versus nurture" debate has been that a gauntlet had been thrown to those who espouse genetic underpinnings to behavior: "show us the relevant genes".

The slow progress of unraveling of the genetic basis of personality is the subject of a recent review article by Jang and colleagues [2]. They point out the lack of any genetic framework in the classification of the Diagnostics and Statistical Manual of American psychiatry (DSM-IV), and the pressing need to identify "genetically crisp" characteristics — or genetic traits of behavior that are independent of competing genetic and environmental influences.

The NPA model posits narcissism to be a genetic trait, being related to the parasympathetic branch of the autonomic nervous system, just as aggression is classically related to the sympathetic branch. This concept of narcissism, and the associated narcissistic rage, is not found in any branch of classical medicine or psychiatry and remains a key point requiring validation. Of note is the recent study by Livesley and colleagues [3] with identical and fraternal twins. They found that of a total of eighteen dimensions of personality it was narcissism that had the highest heritability.

The manuscript of the NPA model was copyrighted with the Library of Congress in 1982, being published in book form in 1985 [17] and in a peer-reviewed journal in 1990 [6]. A revised electronic edition in pdf format was released in 2004 and the online NPA personality test in 2005. Studies are in progress utilizing the NPA personality test in obstetric and gynecological patients [18].

Although the NPA model is several decades old, it has not been validated in the sense of withstanding scrutiny by the scientific method — as is true of all other theories of personality as well. Given the recent advances in deciphering the human genome, such scrutiny may soon be possible. The ideas of Karen Horney have been resilient over time, and the validity of her observations that form the basis of the NPA model awaits the relevant studies in the realm of behavioral genetics.

References

Benis, A.M. *Toward Self and Sanity: On the genetic origins of the human character*, Psychological Dimensions, New York, 1985. ISBN 0884370747 [2nd edition, *The NPA Theory of Personality*, 2017. ISBN 9781521283295]

Benis, A.M. and J.H. Rand (1986). A model of human personality based on Mendelian genetics (abstract). *Proceedings of the American Association for the Advancement of Science,* Publication 86-5, 124.

Benis, A.M. (1990). A theory of personality traits leads to a genetic model for borderline types and schizophrenia. *Speculations in Science and Technology 13* (3), 167-175.

Freud, Sigmund. "Heredity and the aetiology of the neuroses," in *Early Psycho-analytic Publications,* Hogarth, London, [1896] 1962.

Horney, Karen. *Neurosis and Human Growth*, Norton, 1950.

Horney, Karen. *Our Inner Conflicts*, Norton, 1945.

Horney, Karen. *New Ways in Psychoanalysis*, Norton, 1939.

Horney, Karen. *Feminine Psychology*, Norton, [1922 to 1937] 1967.

Jang, K.L., Vernon, P.A. and W.J. Livesley (2001). Behavioural-genetic perspectives on personality function. *Canadian Journal of Psychiatry 46*, 234-244.

Livesley, W.J., Jang, K.L., Jackson, D.N. and P.A. Vernon (1993). Genetic and environmental contributions to dimensions of personality disorder. *American Journal of Psychiatry 150*, 1826-1831.

Stone, Michael H. *The Borderline Syndromes*, McGraw-Hill, 1980.

Citations

1. *Personality*, in Wikipedia.

2. Jang *et al.* (2001). Behavioural-genetic perspectives.

3. Livesley *et al.* (1993). Genetic and environmental contributions.

4. Horney, *Neurosis and Human Growth*, Chapter 8: The expansive solutions: the appeal of mastery.

5. Horney, *Neurosis and Human Growth*, Chapter 4: Neurotic pride.

6. Benis (1990). Theory of personality traits leads to genetic model.

7. Horney, *New Ways in Psychoanalysis*, Chapter 5: The concept of narcissism.

8. Horney, *Our Inner Conflicts*, Chapter 4: Moving against people.

9. Horney, *Feminine Psychology*, pp. 182-213.

10. Horney, *New Ways in Psychoanalysis*, p. 97.

11. Horney, *Our Inner Conflicts*, Chapter 12: Sadistic trends.

12. Horney, *New Ways in Psychoanalysis*, Chapter 15: Masochistic phenomena.

13. Horney, *Our Inner Conflicts*, Chapter 3: Moving toward people.

14. Horney, *Our Inner Conflicts*, Chapter 5: Moving away from people.

15. Horney, *Neurosis and Human Growth*, Chapter 10: Morbid dependency.

16. Benis, *Toward Self and Sanity*, Chapter 10: Genetics.

17. Benis, *Toward Self and Sanity*.

18. by Donna K. Hobgood, M.D., Clinical Attending Physician, University of Tennessee College of Medicine, Chattanooga.

Illustrations

Karen Horney: "Studio photo" courtesy of Karen Horney Papers, Manuscripts and Archives, Yale University Library, New Haven. Copyright unknown.

Character types according to theory of humors: From Johann Kaspar Lavater, *Physiognomics*, ca. 1775.

Olive baboon: U.S. Fish and Wildlife Service.

Source

This article originally appeared in *Wikipedia*, the online encyclopedia in May 2006. It was later deleted for reasons of non-notability. The reference was: "NPA personality theory", *Wikipedia, The Free Encyclopedia*, 2 July 2006, Wikimedia Foundation:
http://en.wikipedia.org/wiki/NPA_personality_theory

GLOSSARY

aggressive rage (A rage)   Mass discharge of the sympathetic nervous system related to the A trait of aggression.

allele   An alternative form of a gene at a given locus

association   The occurrence together, in a family or population, of two characteristics in a frequency greater than that predicted by chance.

autosomal   Pertaining to a non-sex chromosome.

blushing   A response of flushing in an emotional context, in the skin of the face, neck and upper chest. According to the model, individuals having the N trait have an increased predisposition to blushing and flushing.

Borderline type   An NPA type in which neither trait N nor A is fully expressed.

breed true   A trait is said to breed true if two parents of the same phenotype always produce offspring of that same phenotype exclusively. The NA type is the only type of the model that always breeds true: any two NA types can have only NA offspring.

carrier   An individual who carries a gene that is not expressed. In the model, the non-aggressive N and NP types can be carriers of the recessive gene **a** of the trait of aggression.

chromosomes   The cell structures containing the genetic material DNA.   The human genome is composed of 46 chromosomes: 22 pairs of autosomes and 2 sex chromosomes.

cognition   The acts of thinking, feeling, knowing, reasoning and learning, including both awareness and judgment.

complementary genes   Genes that produce different phenotypic effects depending on whether they are present separately or together.

dominant trait   Refers to Mendelian dominance. Not to be confused with *Dominant type*.

Dominant type   An NPA type in which the traits N and/or A are fully expressed. The six types are: N, A, NA, NP, PA and NPA.

ectomorph   Tall and lean *somatotype,* as described by psychologist William Sheldon in the 1940's.

epistasis   The condition in which a gene at one locus suppresses the expression of a gene at another locus.

expressivity   The degree to which a genetic trait is observed in the phenotype. Variable expressivity may be caused by modifier genes or by environmental effects.

extrovert   An individual whose attention and interests are directed primarily toward others.

"fight-or-fight" reaction   Behavioral response associated with mass discharge of the sympathetic nervous system. See also: *aggressive rage.*

gene   A fundamental unit of heredity, composed mainly of DNA. Genes are arranged in linear order on the chromosomes.

genetic heterogeneity   When a similar phenotype can have more than one underlying genetic structure.

genotype   The genetic description of alleles in an individual with respect to a gene locus or loci.

gingival smile   A broad social smile, revealing the gums of the upper teeth, related to the N trait.

heterozygous   Having non-identical alleles at a locus of a homologous pair of chromosomes.

homozygous   Having identical alleles at a locus of a pair of chromosomes.

hybrid   An individual whose parents belong to two different varieties of a species, or to two different species.

introvert   An individual whose interests are predominantly concerned with his own mental life.

lethal gene   A gene that renders non-viable an organism or cell possessing it. According to the present model, the genes corresponding to the absence of traits N and A, when present together, act as *complementary genes* to produce a lethal effect (a non-viable zygote). See the Appendix.

modifier genes   Genes that modify an observed physical or behavioral trait.

mutation   A change in the DNA structure of a gene. If the change occurs in a gamete (reproductive cell), then the alteration may be perpetuated in subsequent generations.

narcissism   From Narcissus, the figure in Greek mythology who fell in love with his own reflected image. In the present model, narcissism is related to the *unbridled* N trait of sanguinity.

narcissistic arms gesture   A gesture of recognition in which the arms are extended to the front or sides, with the fingers slightly spread apart.

narcissistic personality disorder (NPD)   In the NPA model, patients diagnosed with NPD will likely be individuals having the *unbridled* N trait.

narcissistic rage (N rage)   Mass discharge of the autonomic nervous system related to the N trait of sanguinity.

non-sanguine   Refers to individuals who lack the trait N.

Occam's razor   The explanation most likely to be correct is the one that explains the greatest number of observations with the fewest number of assumptions. Also called the principle of parsimony.

Passive Aggressive type   An NPA type in which trait A is genetically partially inhibited.

penetrance   The expression of a trait when the genotype is present. Thus, in "incomplete penetrance" a certain proportion of individuals will not exhibit the trait although the appropriate genotype is present.

perfectionism   The P trait of the model, appearing in behavior as 1) the achievement of order by persistence and repetition, and 2) as a trait that modulates the expression of the unbridled N and A traits.

phenocopy   A phenotype in which environmental factors result in a trait similar to one caused by a genetic mechanism.

phenotype   The observable traits in an individual. The NPA character types (N, NP, NPA, PA, etc.) are phenotypes.

pleiotropism   The determination of multiple characteristics by a single gene.

polygenic   Referring to the influence of several genes determining the expression of a trait.

recessive trait   Refers to a trait that is expressed only when the causative gene is present in the *homozygous* state, i.e., identical alleles on both chromosomes of an autosomal pair.

Resigned type   An NPA type in which trait A is partially inhibited due to environmental stress after maturity.

sadism   Satisfaction derived from aggressively dominating or abusing others.

sadomasochism   A symbiotic relationship of dominance and submission between two individuals based on the trait of aggression.

sanguine, sanguinity   According to ancient physiology, belonging to one of the "four temperaments" in which blood predominates over the other three "humors", leading to a ruddy countenance and exuberant behavior. In the NPA model a sanguine personality type is any type having the genetic N trait.

Submissive type   A compliant Passive Aggressive character type who adopts a life style of deference to others.

somatotype   Classification of physique (body types) developed by psychologist William Sheldon in the 1940's.

temperament   The general level of activity, reactivity or excitability of an individual in the Pavlovian sense.

unbridled trait   The presence of fully expressed trait N or A without modulation by the P trait.

zygote   A fertilized egg that develops into a fetus.

REFERENCES & NOTES

Chapter 1: Personality and Physical Stature

[*1*] See the Appendix: *NPA Personality Theory: Synopsis.* This article, originally published in Wikipedia, is a concise summary of the NPA model.

[*Note to Fig. 2*] If the parents are both NPA×N, and the bride and groom are NP types, then the latter must both be of genotype (**nnPA$_0$a**) and their children would be NP, N, NPA and NA types in the theoretical ratio of 9:3:3:1, respectively, or 9 of 16 children would be tall NP types.

Chapter 2: The NPA Model of Personality

[*2*] In Horney's last book, *Neurosis and Human Growth* (1950), she presents her concept of three "expansive types": "the narcissistic, the perfectionistic and the arrogant-vindictive".

[*3*] Benis (1985/2017). The gingival smile is also seen in other Primates, including the great apes and some Old World monkeys, implying that it has deep evolutionary roots.

[*4*] The caricatures were originally published in Benis (1985/2017). They have been updated in a monograph: Benis (2017b): *Caricatures of the NPA Personality Types.*

[*5*] We wrote in 1985 (Benis A.M., Chap. 11 in *Toward Self & Sanity: On the genetic origins of the human character*, Psychological Dimensions, New York):

> **"Q. Some years ago W. H. Sheldon postulated that there exists a correlation between body habitus (somatotype) and personality. Did you find any such correlation?**
>
> A. Sheldon's point of departure was the occurrence of three basic somatotypes, namely the *endomorph* (obese), the *ectomorph* (lean) and the *mesomorph* (muscular). It is true that certain types do appear frequently, for example the diminutive A type, the portly NPA type, and the ectomorphic NP type — sometimes of Marfanoid proportions. However, exceptions abound, and at best there probably exist loose statistical correlations between character type and somatotype.
>
> Correlations between character type and somatotype could stem from two major sources. First, the genes **n**, **P** and **a** could themselves directly influence morphologic attributes on which somatotype depends. Secondly, in a given population the genes **n**, **P** and **a** could be in linkage disequilibrium with the genes determining somatotype..."

Chapter 3: NPA Types

[*6*] Benis A.M. (2017a).

[*7*] In the NPA model, the A type appears as a "mirror image" of the NP type, in the sense that neither type has any of the NPA traits of the other. Interestingly enough, we found that A types (non-sanguine individuals commonly present in Eastern Europe and the Middle East) were often of *short stature*. Thus, the NP type (of genotype PA_0) tends to be of tall stature, while the A type (which has neither P nor A_0) tends to be of short stature. See ahead, Chapters 4 and 6.

The question arises: does the NPA model predict any possible parental matches where neither parent is an A type, but all of the children are A types? If this occurred, then it might be the basis for families where neither parent is of short stature but all of the children were short. The short answer is "no". As can be seen from Table 5, there are no possible parental matches that this would occur. If neither parent is an A type, then at least one of the parents would have to be a PA type, and irrespective of the NPA type of the matching parent, some of the children would need to have the P trait. The closest approximation to the situation where "neither parent is an A type, but the children are A types" would be the match PA×PA, where the children could be 75% PA types and 25% A types, with no problems of infertility. This is a match of two non-sanguine types and would be uncommon in most areas of the world, but would certainly occur in Eastern Europe and the Middle East. In our experience, most PA types are not especially tall, not standing out in the crowd.

Chapter 4: Inheritance of the NPA Traits

[*8*] Benis (1985/2017). The unusual mechanism of transmission for N and A, as high-frequency *recessive* traits, leads to the hypothesis that these loci code for inhibitors of the traits, and that an inactive inhibitor would lead to a "release of inhibition" allowing expression of that trait. For trait A, the model implies that whatever the complexity of the many possible genes that permit the expression and modulation of the trait of aggression, it is a single genetic locus (the A_0 allele of the NPA model) that permits inhibition of the final common pathway to expression of the A trait and A rage, permitting the occurrence of the non-aggressive N and NP types of the model. For trait N, the model implies that whatever the complexity of the genes that permit the expression and modulation of the trait of sanguinity, it is a single genetic locus (the N_0 allele) that permits inhibition of the final common pathway to

expression of the N trait and N rage, permitting the occurrence of the non-sanguine A and PA types.

Note that in this book we mostly use the recessive alleles **n** and **a,** rather than their matched dominant alleles N_0 and A_0 that are assumed to code for the absence of traits N and A, respectively.

[9] For details of Passive Aggressive types, in whom trait A is genetically partially inhibited, see the Appendix. In this book, in the interests of brevity, we omit the possibility of a Passive Aggressive NPA− type or a Borderline PA− type as a parent in those case examples where one of the parents is a Dominant NPA or PA type, respectively (see Chap. 6).

[*10*] In the category of *partial infertility,* one such parental combination would be a match of the genotypes **(nP/nP)×(nPa/Pa),** which would correspond to a mating NP×PA. Theoretically, fifty percent of the issue would be of genotype **(nP/Pa),** hence non-viable. In the category of *complete infertility,* an example would be the match **(n/nP)×(a/Pa),** which would again correspond to a mating NP×PA. Such a union could give issue only to non-viable progeny of genotype **(na)**, i.e., null type, or **(nPa)** and **(nPPa),** i.e., P types.

Chapter 7: Conclusion

[*11*] Wahlsten D. (2012).

BIBLIOGRAPHY

Benis A.M. (1985). *Toward Self & Sanity: On the genetic origins of the human character,* Psychological Dimensions, New York. Revised edition (2017), as *NPA Theory of Personality*, New York, KDP/Amazon.

Benis A.M. (2017a). *Geographic Distribution of Genetic Character Traits Based on the NPA Theory of Personality*, KDP/Amazon.

Benis A.M. (2017b). *Caricatures of the NPA Personality Types*, KDP/Amazon.

Benis A.M. (2017c). *How Your Personality Type Is Inherited: The NPA Model of Genetic Traits*, KDP/Amazon.

Benis A.M. (2017d). *NPA Personality Theory: The Essentials,* KDP/Amazon.

Benis A.M. (2017e). *NPA Personality Theory in Images,* KDP/Amazon.

Benis A.M. (1990). A theory of personality traits leads to a genetic model for borderline types and schizophrenia. *Speculations in Science and Technology* 13 (3), 167-75.

Dobzhansky T. (1970). *Genetics of the Evolutionary Process.* Columbia University Press, New York.

Horney K. (1950). *Neurosis and Human Growth*, Norton, New York.

Orr H.A. (1995). The population genetics of speciation: The evolution of hybrid incompatibilities, *Genetics* 139, 1805-13.

Orr H.A. (1995a). Dobzhansky, Bateson and the genetics of speciation, *Genetics* 144, 1331-35.

Wahlsten D. (2012). The hunt for gene effects pertinent to behavioral traits and psychiatric disorders: From mouse to human, *Dev Psychobiol* 54, 475-92.

SOURCES OF ILLUSTRATIONS

Figure 1, p. 4:

The four characters of man, from Johann Kaspar Lavater (*ca.* 1775): *Physiognomics*.

Figure 2, p. 6:

Bridal couple with their parents, by Katherine Hala. Creative Commons license via: flickr.com/photos/kahala/4501198519.

Figure 3, p. 10:

Gingival smile, by max_thinks_sees. Creative Commons license via: flickr.com/photos/hundreds/2830576097.

Figure 4, p. 12:

Faces in rage, By Anthony Moore, from Desmond Morris (1977): *Manwatching*. Courtesy of Elsevier/Equinox Publishing Projects, Oxford.

Figure 5, p. 16:

Barack Obama by DonkeyHotey. Creative Commons license via Wikipedia Commons File: 2012 Obama Romney caricature.jpg.

Vladimir Putin by DonkeyHotey. Creative Commons license via: Wikipedia Commons File: Vladimir Putin - Olympic Host.jpg.

Angela Merkel by DonkeyHotey. Creative Commons license via: flickr.com/photos/donkeyhotey/12952652895.

Richard Cheney by DonkeyHotey. Creative Commos license via: flickr.com/photos/donkeyhotey/16011605976.

Christopher Christie by DonkeyHotey. Creative Commons license via: flickr.com/photos/donkeyhotey/9529109477.

Adele Adkins. Digital painting by Carsten S., Berlin, Germany. Creative Commons license via: flickr.com/photos/caschie/25600151946.

Figure 6, p. 22: Abraham Lincoln vs Zombies, by Bill Oberst Jr. Creative Commos license via: flickr.com/photos/billoberstjr/6940092689.

ACKNOWLEDGEMENT

With thanks to my colleague, Jacob H. Rand, M.D., who provided invaluable assistance with the original version of the NPA model and helped to guide the manuscript to the publisher.

ABOUT THE AUTHOR

The author received the degree of Doctor of Science from MIT. His medical training was at the Mount Sinai Medical Center in New York, where he served afterward for many years as Research Associate Professor and Director of Cardiothoracic Intensive Care. He is the author of a number of research papers and review articles. His interest in the genetics of personality grew with his experience with families in the intensive care environment.